RESTAURANT MANAGEMENT CONFIDENTIAL

COMPREHENSIVE GUIDE FOR RESTAURANT PROFESSIONALS

GAJANAN SHIRKE

Made with ♥ on the Notion Press Platform
www.notionpress.com

Dedicated to all food and beverage service professionals

Contents

Acknowledgements

I would like to express a special debt of gratitude to my wife Rajeshree and my two daughters Rupeshi & Kavya, my well-wishers and teammates for their support and guidance.

About Book

Restaurant Management Confidential is focused on both understanding and performing, its goal is to provide students and working professional with a solid theoretical and practical foundation in restaurant practices to strengthen their skills and ready reference for creating front-of-house ambience and back-of-house efficiencies.

About The Author

Gajanan Shirke, a hotel consultant, has years of extensive experience in the hospitality industry. His thirst for learning and aspiration to become a multi-faceted expert in the hotel industry helped him rise from employment to becoming an independent professional in the hospitality sector. Since his last assignment as General Manager at Kamat Hotels, he has become a renowned hotel consultant with a proven track record of developing, training and growing some of the best-known hotels, restaurants and fast-food joints in the Indian market. He was appointed as an expert consultant for The Eighth meeting of the Board of Studies for Hotel Management & Catering Technology. He is a visiting faculty at various Hotel Management Colleges and has trained over a thousand hospitality professionals. He has completed numerous pre and post opening hotel consultancies in India and overseas.

In order to spread his extensive knowledge to aspiring hotel professionals, Gajanan has penned a large number of books spanning different segments of the hospitality industry. Starting from his first book 'Bar Management and Operations' published in 2010, he has written 39 books including Hospitality Management, Food and Beverage Management, Hotel Engineering Management, Front Office Management, Hotel Housekeeping Management, The Cookery Trilogy: Advance Cookery Theory, The Cookery Trilogy: Foundation of Cookery, The Cookery Trilogy: The Basic Cookery Book, Hotel Sales and Marketing, Hospitality Industry Accounting & Fundamentals, Customer Interaction Excellence in Hospitality, History of Indian Cuisine – Volume 1, History of Indian Cuisine – Volume 2, Hotel Owner's Manual, Hotel Security & Prevention, Training Manager's Manual, Exceptional Service In Hospitality Six Sigma Way, etc.

Index

CHAPTER ONE

Restaurant Basics

Effective restaurant management involves several challenges, such as public relations, inventory, staff, and customer service. In some instances, a restaurant owner may also serve as the manager. Either way, a strong manager is an essential component of a successful restaurant—they are usually the person who handles both staff and customer issues. The following information explains the important basics for properly managing a restaurant.

Casual dining restaurants: Casual dining restaurants serve food à la carte at moderate prices with full-table service. Casual dining restaurants—whether they are chains or independently owned—cover a wide variety of cuisines, including Mexican, American, Italian, and Chinese.

Fine dining restaurants: Fine dining restaurants offer attentive, full table service in a more formal dining room setting than a casual restaurant. The food at fine dining restaurants is often considered higher-quality, more expensive than casual dining restaurants, and often involves meals with several courses including wine or cocktails, appetizers, salads, entrées, side dishes, and desserts. A fine dining restaurant may require you to dress up in accordance with the restaurant's dress code.

Family-style restaurants: Family-style restaurants serve large portions of moderately-priced food meant to be shared by large parties. These types of restaurants typically offer table service in a laid-back atmosphere. Some cuisines well-suited to family-style dining include Italian-American food, Chinese-American food, and traditional American food because these cuisines often include large, shareable portions of dishes like pasta, noodles, stir-fries, and fried finger food.

Fast-casual restaurants: Fast-casual restaurants typically offer counter service instead of table service. These eateries either allow customers to order items from a menu, or to build their own customizable meals at the counter. Fast-casual restaurants commonly serve sandwiches, burgers, burritos, and salads. This type of dining experience has become increasingly popular because it balances the quality of casual dining with the speed of fast food.

Fast-food restaurants: A fast-food restaurant is a type of quick-service-restaurant (or QSR) that serves low-cost food quickly from a counter or drive-through. Fast food restaurants offer a fixed menu of mass-produced food that is usually pre-cooked to expedite service. Many fast-food chains have international locations and are some of the most popular restaurants around the world.

Food trucks: Food trucks serve moderately-priced food that is made-to-order from a full kitchen inside of a vehicle. They usually only offer counter service and don't often have seating. Food trucks typically specialize in one particular type of food item like tacos, barbecue, hot dogs, grilled cheese, or ice cream. Food trucks usually drive to new locations that are convenient for their customers—like offices, flea markets, or private events. Food trucks are a great way for entrepreneurs to test a new restaurant concept because they require fewer staff members and less overhead than a brick-and-mortar location.

Pop-up restaurants: Pop-up restaurants are dining establishments that open in a specific location for a limited period of time. They can involve counter service or table service and usually have limited seating. A benefit to a pop-up restaurant is that it allows chefs and business owners to test out a dining concept for a limited period of time without making a huge real estate commitment and leasing a brick-and-mortar space.

Bars and pubs: A bar or pub is an establishment that primarily serves alcohol, and sometimes offers a limited food menu consisting of casual dishes like finger foods and burgers. Bartenders typically take food orders from the bar when you submit your drink order. Certain fine dining and casual dining establishments include a self-seating bar area, but bars can also be standalone establishments.

Cafés: Cafés provide counter service with a wide range of coffee items including espressos, cappuccinos, and lattes. Casual food items like sandwiches, salads, and pastries are sometimes served as well.

Buffets: Buffet-style restaurants offer customizable plates at a fixed price per person. In a buffet-style restaurant, customers serve themselves, choosing from a variety of food items laid out on a bar or row of tables. Buffets sometimes offer all-you-can-eat options, and customers can return to the bar for multiple rounds of food.

Restaurant Categorization Factors

We can distinguish restaurants from one another by a variety of elements. Below are the broadest and most common factors people use to categorize restaurants:

Formality Spectrum. The decor of a restaurant, along with how guests are expected to dress, determines how casual or upscale an eatery is. In addition, table service versus counter service and the attentiveness of the servers are also indicators.

Fine dining: high-end decor, formal dress, full table service, and attentive servers

Casual restaurants: relaxed atmosphere, casual dress, full table service, counter service, or less formal servers

Price. Restaurants fall under a price range of inexpensive to quite pricey. Google uses dollar signs to denote the average price of a meal at its business listings, providing a convenient way to look at restaurant pricing:

Food. Restaurants further differ as a result of each establishment's type, quality, and presentation of food.

Type of Food: Menus may be based on a cuisine from a certain region, or they may solely feature innovations from the chef. Other restaurants might devise menus based on specific types of food, as pizzerias and steakhouses do, or according to certain diets, like plant-based ones.

Quality of Ingredients: Quality relates to what the ingredients are, where they're from, and how they are prepared. For example, a restaurant may solely utilize fresh, local, and organic ingredients. On the other hand, an eatery might use processed food made with preservatives. A restaurant might employ a made-to-order, deliberate preparation process, or it may prepare large quantities quickly in bulk.

Presentation of Meals: Some restaurants feature highly aesthetic dishes with garnishes, whereas other restaurants utilize a more modest, simple presentation. Some restaurants only serve food in disposable take-out items and others serve on the finest dinnerware.

It's possible to distinguish restaurants from one another based on common categorization factors. Additionally, restaurants differentiate themselves from one another based on each one's unique brand.

Restaurants Have Fixed or Flexible Categorization Factors

Some types of restaurants have fixed factors, while others are subject to change. For example, fine dining establishments are almost always formal and pricey, whereas fast food and casual restaurants are usually more affordable options with laid-back environments. On the other hand, a family style restaurant or a pop-up restaurant might be casual and moderately priced, but you may also find one that is upscale and pricey.

Restaurants are usually conceptualized by the way they employ the different elements, but many of these elements do partner together often.

CHAPTER TWO

Restaurant Service Styles

Restaurants are classified into three primary categories: quick-service, midscale and upscale. Quick-service restaurants are also known as fast-food restaurants. These establishments offer limited menus of items that are prepared quickly and sold for a relatively low price. In addition to very casual dining areas, they typically offer drive-thru windows and take-out service. When people think of fast-food restaurants, they often think of burgers and french fries, but establishments in this category also serve chicken, hot dogs, sandwiches, pizza, seafood and ethnic foods.

To open a restaurant, you not only determine the type of food menu, but also need to consider various aspects, ranging from the interior, atmosphere, to the type of service. Now, in today's digital era, we can find various types of services in restaurants. As your inspiration, let's look at 4 types of service at the dining place that you can apply!

Self-service: Usually, we can meet the waiter at the restaurant who will help us to order food and make payments. This type of service is called full service. However, nowadays, many eating places have also begun to implement self-service methods. Customers who come will serve their own needs, ranging from selecting menus, taking food or drinks, making transactions, to clean the equipment after he finished eating the food menu.

Table service: In addition to self service, we can also apply the method of table service, where customers who come will first enter the restaurant and choose their own seats. After that, then there are waiters who record orders and bring their food. In this type of service, there are also service options such as family service that involves the business owner to serve his guests at his own restaurant.

Assisted service: This type of assisted service is an application of semi self-service. The customer who comes to the assisted service will take the food he wants, then he will make the payment at the cashier. After that, the food will be processed and served by the waiter at the restaurant.

Special service: The type of service at a place to eat which is also now commonly found is special service, where businesses provide special services to food and beverage delivery service providers. Some of them are like home delivery, on-flight tray service, lounge service with comfortable special rooms, and room service that is widely available in hotels. Not only that, special service can also be found in the grill room restaurants..

Broadly we can categories the service methods into five types:

Table Service
Assisted service
Self-service
Single point service
Specialised or in situ service

Table Service

In this category, the guest enters in the area and is seated. Menu lists are given or displayed for orders. The orders are been taken by waiter/ess. Then the service is done using a laid cover on the table. The following are types of service come under this category:

English Service: Often referred to as the "Host Service" because the host plays an active role in the service. Food is brought on platters by the waiter and is shown to the host for approval. The waiter then places the platters on the tables. The host either portions the food onto the guest plates directly or portions the food and allows the waiter to serve. For replenishment of guest food the waiter may then take the dishes around for guests to help themselves or be served by the waiter.

French Service: It is a very personalized service. Food is brought from the kitchen in dishes and salvers, which are placed directly on the table. The plates are kept near the dish and the guests help themselves.

Silver Service: The table is set for hors d'oeuvres, soup, main courses and sweet dish in sterling silverware. The food is portioned into silver platters at the kitchen itself, which are placed at the sideboard with burners or hot plates to keep the food warm in the restaurant. Plates are placed before the guest. The waiter then picks the platter from the hot plate and presents the dish to the host for approval. He serves each guest using a service spoon and fork. All food is presented in silver dishes with elaborate dressing.

American/Plate Service: The American service is a pre-plated service, which means that the food is served into the guest's plate in the kitchen itself and brought to the guest. The kitchen predetermines the portion and the accompaniments served with the dish and then balance the entire presentation in terms of nutrition and colour. This type of service is commonly used in a coffee shop where service is required to be fast.

Russian Service: An elaborate silver service thought to be the foundation of French service except that the food is portioned and carved by the waiter at the gueridon trolley in the restaurant in full view of the guests. Display and theatrical presentation are a major part of this service. The principle involved is to have whole joints, poultry, game and fish elaborately dressed and garnished, presented to guests and carved and portioned by the waiter.

Gueridon Service: This is a service where a dish comes partially prepared from the kitchen to be completed in the restaurant by the waiter or when a complete meal is cooked at the tableside in the restaurant. The cooking is done on a gueridon trolley, which is a mobile trolley with a gas cylinder and burners.

The waiter plays a prominent part, as he is required to fillet, carve, flambé and prepare the food with showmanship. The waiter has to have considerable dexterity and skill.

Snack-bar Service: Tall stools are placed along a counter so that the guest may eat the food at the counter itself. In better establishments, the covers are laid out on the counter itself. Food is either displayed behind the counter for the guests to choose from, or is listed on a menu card or simple blackboard.

Assisted Service

In this type of category, the guest enters the dining area and helps himself to the food, either from a buffet counter or he may get served partly at the table by waiter/ess and he collects any extras he needs from the counter. Eating may be done either at the table, standing or in the lounge area/ banquet hall.

- **Buffet Service**: A self-service, where food is displayed on tables. The guest takes his plate from a stack at the end of each table or requests the waiter behind the buffet table to serve him. For sit-down buffet service, tables are laid with crockery and cutlery as in a restaurant. The guest may serve himself at the buffet table and return to eat at the guest table laid out. The waiter may serve a few courses like the appetizer and soup at the table.

Self Service

In this type of service, the guest enters the dining area, selects his own tray or from the food counter and carries food by himself to his seating place.

- **Cafeteria Service**: This service exists normally in industrial canteens, colleges, hospitals or hotel cafeterias. To facilitate quick service, the menu is fixed and is displayed on large boards. The guest may have to buy coupons in advance and present them to the counter waiter who

then serves the desired item. Sometimes food is displayed behind the counter and the guests may indicate their choice to the counter attendant. The food is served pre-plated and the cutlery is handed directly to the guest. Guests may then sit at tables and chairs provided by the establishment. Sometimes high tables are provided where guests can stand and eat.

Single Point Service

In this category, the guest pays for his order and gets served all at a single point. There may or may not be any dining area or seats. The different types are:

Take Away: Customer orders and is served from a single point, at the counter, hatch or snack stand; customer consumes off the premises.

Vending: Provision of food service and beverage service by means of automatic retailing.

Kiosks: Outstation to provide service for peak demand or in a specific location (maybe open for customers to order or used for dispensing only).

Food Court: series of autonomous counters where customers may either order and eat or buy from a number of counters and eat in the separate eating areas, or take-away.

Specialised Service

In this category, the guest is served at a place, which is not meant or designated for food & beverage service (i.e. guest rooms or any special area).

Grill Room Service: In this form of service various meats are grilled in front of the guest. The meats may be displayed behind a glass partition or well-decorated counter so that the guest can select his exact cut of meat. The food comes pre-plated.

Tray service: Method of service of whole or part of the meal on a tray to the customer in situ, e.g. hospitals aircraft or railway catering.

Trolley service: Method of service of food and beverages from the trolley, away from dining areas, e.g. for office workers, in aircraft or on trains.

Home-Delivery: Food delivered to customer's home or place of work, e.g. Pizza home delivery or Meal on wheels etc.

Lounge Service: Service of a variety of foods and beverages in lounge area.

Room Service: It implies serving of food and beverage in guest rooms of hotels. Small orders are served in trays. Major meals are taken to the room on trolleys. The guest places his order with the room service order taker. The waiter receives the order and transmits the same to the kitchen. In the meanwhile, he prepares his tray or trolley. He then goes to the cashier to have a check prepared to take along with the food order for the guests' signature or payment. Usually, clearance of soiled dishes from the room is done after half an hour or an hour. However, the guest can telephone Room Service for clearance as and when he has finished with the meal. There are two types of Room Service:

Centralized room service: Here al the food orders are processed from the main kitchen and sent to the rooms by a common team of waiters.

Decentralized room service: Each floor or a set of floor may have separate pantries to service them. Orders are taken at a central point by order-takers who in turn convey the order to the respective pantry.

Breakfast

Breakfast: Breakfast service must be quick, prompt, and cheerful. Many patrons are not morning people and are grumpy until they've at least had their first cup of coffee, and others do not cheer up until they have had their breakfast. All breakfast foods need to be served at the appropriate temperature, so prompt service from the kitchen to the table is vital. Do not wait for your guest to finish the first course of their breakfast before bringing the hot entrée.

- Fresh fruit or fruit juice is usually the first course for breakfast and it is served first, with the dishes or glasses removed before the next course, which might be cereal.
- This course is then removed prior to bringing out the hot entrée.
- Coffee is placed to the right of the spoons.

- Finger bowls can sometimes be used for breakfast service. If fruit may have stained your customer's fingers, these are served immediately after the fruit course; otherwise it is offered at the end of the meal.
- The check is presented face down to the right of the *cover* or on a clean tray.

Lunch

Lunch: Lunch guests are categorized into two groups: business people, who have a short period of time for lunch and need to be served quickly, and the shoppers, ladies' groups, or travelers, who have more opportunity for a leisurely lunch period. Your biggest job here is to serve those who need to eat quickly with prompt service while not rushing the second group of individuals.

- Beverage is always first, usually ice water.
- Chilled butter is placed on a cold bread and butter plate.
- All foods are placed in the center of the *cover* and then removed when finished.
- The only exceptions are the salad plates, which are placed to the left of the forks, about two inches from the edge of the table, and the bread/rolls, which are placed to the left of the salad plate.
- Hot beverages are placed to the right of the cup and saucer, with creamer above the cup.

- If dessert is ordered, *crumb* the table first. This means you use a small device to remove any crumbs left from the bread or entrée that have landed on the cloth in front of your guest.
- Place dessert silver to the right of the *cover*, place the dessert plate in the center of the cover.
- Serve hot beverages as requested.
- Remove the dessert plate when your guests are finished.
- Serve finger bowls.
- Lastly, present the check face down.

Dinner

Dinner: Most dinner patrons are looking for a dining experience and will not be in a great hurry. While they may not be in a hurry, it is necessary to avoid any long waits between courses, which will annoy your guests. Be very observant without hovering.

- Serving from the left, place the appetizer service on the center of the *cover*.
- If a tray will be offered for the guest to serve himself, an empty appetizer plate must be placed in front of him first.
- Remove the appetizer dishes.
- Place the soup or salad service on the center of the cover.
- All service from a course is to be removed prior to bringing out the next course.
- If the entrée is served on a platter, it is placed directly above the *cover* with serving silver to the right.
- A warm dinner plate is placed on the cover. Or, if the entrée is served *Russian service* style, then the plated entrée is placed on the cover.

- Salad is placed to the left of the forks when it is served with the entrée.
- Beverages are placed to the right of the teaspoons.
- Rolls are placed to the left of the salad plate.
- If salad is served as a separate course, it will follow the main course. Place a salad fork to the left of the cover and the salad in the center of the cover. When finished, remove salad service.
- Crumb the table.
- Place silver for dessert course and place the dessert service in the center of the cover.
- Hot beverages are placed to the right.

CHAPTER THREE

Restaurant Equipment

Food and beverage service equipment includes all pieces of equipment for the furniture. Cutlery, crockery, glassware, Linen used by the guests and the staff in the service area.

A wide range of food and service equipment is available in the market to suit the requirements of various styles of food service operations. Food and beverage service equipment play an important role to elevate the guest experience to complement the outlet theme and to build the mood of the guests.

Here is a list of food and beverage service equipment

Furniture: Dining room furniture is available in many shapes, sizes, materials, colours, textures, and designs. All of these f&b service equipment must be taken into account while selecting them. So that the furniture blends with the decor of the food service area. Furniture occupies most of the service area, so these should be arranged carefully for maximum space utilization.

Types of F&B furniture

1. **Table**
2. **Chair**
3. **Sideboard**

Table: Restaurant tables are generally divided into two section

A) Tabletops: They come in an assortment of sizes and shapes, of different materials such as wood, mica, glass, and stone. Wooden tops are used in upscale restaurants as they look elegant and rich.

B) Table bases: They are holding posts of the tables and come in a variety of designs that are selected to best match the theme and design of the dining area. Round table bases give a roomier feel underneath.

<u>Chair</u>

A) wood frame chairs: offers a distinct style and brings out a sense of tradition and class to the establishment. Wooden chairs are a favorite among steak houses, family-style, and fine dining restaurants. The natural colours and grain in the wood add a classy and elegant accent to the theme.

B) Metal chairs: will typically project a more modern and sleek look than wooden chairs. Metal restaurant chair are painted and come in a wide variety of seat cover and backrest cover option

C) High chair and booster seats: High chair and booster seats are a necessity in most food service establishments and restaurants for children. High chairs are available in wood and plastic and come in a variety of finishes and colours.

D) Banquet chair: The chairs chosen should be stackable, comfortable, strong and sturdy as they will be transported frequently from place to place.

The standard size of chairs

- Height of the chair (from floor to the seat) 18

- From floor to the top of the chair 39
- Depth of the chair 18

Sideboard (Dummy waiter): Foodservice personnel will not be able to extend quick service and work efficiently without a sideboard. It holds all the necessary cutlery crockery, hollowware, menu card, checks pad, accompanying sauce, that are required during service.

Enter Caption

The following items are kept on the sideboard
Soup spoons
Fish knives and forks
Dessert spoons and forks
Large knives and forks
Service spoon and forks
Tea and coffee spoons

Underliner
Glassware
Napkins
Sugar bowls with tongs
Cups and saucers
Cruets
Ashtrays
Paper napkins
candle stand
trays

Linen: The linen in the foodservice area covers tablecloths, napkins, tray cloths. Slip cloths, buffet cloths, waiter's cloth, and tea cloths

Different types of linen used in food and beverage service/restaurant

Tablecloth
Napkins
Slip cloth
Tray cloth
Buffet cloth
Satin cloth
Tea cloth

Tablecloth: All tables with wooden tops are covered with tablecloths to enhance the dining area. Plain tables can quickly be transformed into formal dining seating with the use of tablecloths. Tablecloths are generally used in fine dining restaurants. The colour of the tablecloth must go well with the colour scheme of the interior.

Napkins: These are for guest use normally kept folded at each cover and unfolded and spread on laps of guests by the service staff or by the guest themselves. Napkins are available in many attractive colours. Each restaurant use napkins of a different colour for proper control.

The standard size of napkins

18 × 18 For lunch
20 × 20 For dinner

Slip cloth: It is used to cover the soiled tablecloths during operations. The size of the cloth should be adequate enough to cover the surface of the table with a fall of a few inches. This cloth is thin as compared to the material of the tablecloth and can be washed frequently.

Waiter,s cloth: It is used by waiters extensively during service. The edges of dishes are wiped with this cloth, when necessary. While carrying dishes to the table, this cloth is folded and kept under the dish.

Tray cloth: All trays and salvers should be lined with tray cloths for better presentation and good grip for items being carried

Buffet cloth: Foodservice operations use buffet cloths of various sizes to cover the buffet tables

Satin cloth: This cloth is draped around the front side of the buffet table, primarily to cover the leg and to make the buffet counter attractive

Tea cloth: This is used exclusively for wiping cutlery and crockery. The cloth should be lint-free and changed frequently.

Crockery: Crockery includes all items of earthenware or chinaware such as plates, cups and saucers, pots, vases. The following are the different types of chinaware available in the market

Different types of crockery in food and beverage service

Earthenware
bone china
Porcelain
Stoneware
Alumina
Melamine
Terracotta

Earthenware: It is made of 25 per cent ball clay, 25 per cent kaolin or clay, 15 per cent china stone, and 35 per cent flint. The advantage of earthenware is that it is cheaper, but it is easily chipped or cracked and much heavier than

Bone china: Bone china It is made of 25 per cent china clay, 25 per cent china stone, and 50 per cent calcium phosphate. It is strong and translucent. It looks beautiful and is very expensive. Nowadays, manufacturers have introduced crockery which has qualities of bone china but is less expensive, such crockery e Available under a variety of trade names such as Vitrex, Vitrock, Steelite, and so on. They are stronger than earthenware and less expensive compared to bone china.

Porcelain: It is made of 50 per cent china clay, 25 per cent quartz, and 25 per cent feldspar (aluminosilicate mineral). It is vitreous and translucent, with a grey or blue tinge. It is used in oven-to-tableware dishes.

Stoneware: It is hard, tough, and vitreous crockery, fired at a high temperature. It is heavy and available in bright colours, suitable for restaurants where bright colour crockery is required.

Alumina: Alumina enriched crockery can normally be spotted due to its creamy colour. Alumina is an oxide of aluminium which is added to the clay to give it additional strength. Though the addition of alumina makes the crockery more expensive than standard porcelain, it is generally cheaper than bone china, making it a popular alternative.

Melamine: Melamine is a strong, lightweight and hard thermosetting plastic. It is used as an ideal hygienic and durable alternative to china. It is virtually unbreakable so is considered for daily use and it can also resist scratching, staining and is dishwasher safe.

Terracotta: Terracotta is a traditional Spanish material often used in both oven & tableware. It has unique properties that react with acidic foods such as tomato sauce, giving natural sweetness to the meal. Its colour can instantly be recognised and is often associated with Mediterranean cooking.

Different types of crockery and their size and use

S.no	Name	Size.	Uses
1.	Quarter plate	6″ D	Bread, cheese, underli for bowls
2.	Half plate/fish plate/dessert plate	8″D	Hord d' oeuvre, fish, pasta, and savoury, sweet, and dessert
3.	Full plate/Dinner plate/joint plate	10″ D	Main course
4.	Soup plate	8″ D	For thick soup and breakfast cereals
5.	Soup cup	250ml	For thin soups, also known as consommé
6.	Soup bowls	250ml	For thick and thin sou breakfast cereals
7.	Breakfast cup	250-300ml	For all tea and coffee served during breakfa
8.	Teacup	200ml	For tea and coffee serv during the day
9.	Demitasse	100ml	For coffee served after lunch and dinner
10.	Saucer	4″ D	Used as an underliner

Enter Caption

Points to be considered while purchasing crockery

- Type of service being offered
- Type of customer
- Design
- Flexibility of use
- Durability
- Ease of maintenance
- Stackability

- Cost and funds available
- Availability in the future-replacements
- Storage
- Shape

- The psychological effect on customers
- Crockery should have a rolled edge which will give added reinforcement at the edge.
- The pattern should be under the glaze because the pattern on top of the glaze will wear out & discolour quickly.

Points should be considered while selecting the chinaware

- Plates should have complete and even glaze.
- Pattern or design should be underglaze so that it is protected and does not wear out with repeated washing.
- Suitable for multiple purposes, for example, using bowls for soups and breakfast cereals, half-plate for the appetizer, fish, vegetables, savoury, and sweet.
- Stackable up to 30 plates or saucers in one pile
- Suitable for machine washing
- Plates should have rolled edge to resist chipping
- Lightweight
- Suitable for microwave application
- Resistant to high temperatures of 85 °C

Glassware: Food and beverage service outlets use a variety of glasses for different types of drinks which call a huge investment in delicate and fragile equipment.

The style, quality, and sparkle of glass selected portray the profile of the restaurant. Glasses are named by the drinks served in though there are many glasses for different drinks, it is better to go for limited types of glasses the may be suitable for all kinds of drinks.

Classification of glassware according to their parts

- Stemware
- footed ware
- Tumbler

Stemware: It is basically a bowl without a stem or foot. Its sides may be straight, widened, or curved. Examples: Rock glass, old-fashioned, highball, Collins, juice glass, and so on

Footed ware: In this type, the bowl sits directly on a base or foot without the stem. Bowl and base may come in a variety of shapes. Examples: brandy balloon, beer goblet.

Stemware: It refers to glasses that have all three parts-bowl, base, and stem. In this type, the stem connects the bowl with the base or foot. Examples: red wine glass, white wine glass, Champagne saucer, Champagne flute, Cocktail glass, and so on.

Tableware: The term tableware refers to all pieces of flatware, cutlery, and hollowware.

Flatware: Flatware in catering parlance means all forms of spoons and forks. However, cutlery is the common term used frequently in the hotel industry to refer to spoons, forks, and knives used for eating.

Cutlery: Cutlery denotes all types of knives and other cutting equipment used in the dining area. Cutlery is available in various designs in silver, and stainless steel material.

Holloware: This refers to all tableware other than cutlery. It includes pots, jugs, platters, a buffet dish, finger bowls, wine chiller, straw holder.

Silverware: The silverware is made of Electro Plated Nickel Silver (EPNS). These are made from an alloy of brass, zinc, stainless steel or nickel with silver plating of 10 to 15 microns. Silverware includes spoons, forks, knives, hollowware, drinkware, tongs, an ice bucket, and a salver.

Type of cutlery:Cutlery implies implements used for cutting and eating food. It includes knife, fork and spoon. There are different types of knives, forks and spoons. A complete cutlery set may include butter knife, soup spoon, seafood fork etc.

Knife: Different knives are designed to serve specific tasks. Choosing the right knife makes it easier to perform that task. A knife can be designed for striking, chopping, tearing, dicing, spreading, carving or slicing. The difference lies in the blade of the knife whether it is pointed, blunt, serrated etc. Dull blades are used to cut soft or cooked food while serrated knives are easy to cut meat. Non-serrated steak knives allow for a cleaner cut while pointed knives help in cutting or paring fruits. Knife with a broad flat blade is suitable for eating fish while knife with blunt ends is used to spread butter, cheese spreads, marmalades etc.

Classification of knives based on size

Dinner knife: Dinner knife is sized between 9 ½ and 10 inches. It is used to cut and push food. It also serves as a replacement for salad knife if latter is not available.

Steak knife: A steak knife can be used in place of dinner knife or in addition to it. It can be serrated or non-serrated depending on specific steak cuts. It is usually four to six inches long.

Luncheon knife: Slightly smaller than dinner knife, luncheon knife is used with luncheon plate to suit the size of the plate. Dinner knife is equally acceptable when luncheon knife is not available.

Fish knife: Fish knife is used when fish is served for dinner. Fish knife measures 8 ¾ inches with a wide blade and dull edge. The tip of fish knife aids in separating layers of fish and lift bones.

Dessert knife: Dessert knife can be used for dessert, fresh or candied fruit. It can be used to cut cakes and pastries. It goes together with the dessert spoon.

Fruit knife

Measuring between 6 ½ and 7 ¼ inches, fruit knife has a pointed tip and a narrow straight. The blade can be serrated or slightly curved. It is meant to cut and peel fruits.

Butter knife: Small in size at 5 to 6 inches, butter knife has a rounded point so that it does not scrape the bread while spreading butter. Dinner knife is equally acceptable if butter knife is not available.

Spoons: Spoons are used to transfer food from platter or bowl to mouth. There are different types of spoon for specific tasks.

Teaspoon: It is meant for stirring coffee, tea, soups and eating.

Tablespoon: A tablespoon is bigger than a teaspoon and is used for serving food from serving bowls.

Place spoon: It is an all-purpose spoon bigger than a teaspoon but smaller than a tablespoon.

Soup spoon: A large rounded spoon used for eating soup. An oval spoon is used in case soup contains meat, vegetables, bread crumbs etc.

Dessert spoon: It is used for eating sweet dishes and puddings.

Sundae spoon: Long spoons to reach the bottom of sundae glass and eat liquid or semi-liquid food like ice-cream toppings, floats, jelly etc.

Fruit spoon: Fruit spoon has an elongated bowl and a pointed tip that aids in cutting fruit and eating fruits like grapes, oranges and melons.

Forks:The two-tined fork is used cut meat while there or four-tined fork has other uses.

Dinner fork: Meant for the main course, dinner fork measures around seven inches.

Salad fork: Used for eating salad, in salad fork outer tines are notched, wider and longer than inner tines. It is six inches in length.

Forks with extra-long tines: Such forks are meant for eating spaghetti, noodles.

Dessert fork: It is used for eating cake, pies and pastries. It is more or less similar to salad fork.

Fish fork: It is used for holding and serving fish. Tines are uniform in width and length.

Sea food fork: Sea food fork is ideal for eating crustaceans. Also called crab fork, lobster fork, it serves two purposes. The double-pronged slim end is used to pick sea food while the curved scraper is used to scoop out the meat.

Choose cutlery carefully

Choosing the right cutlery can be mind-boggling especially if you are a first timer. Bear these quick tips in mind while purchasing cutlery.

- Avoid limited edition cutlery
- Apart from the standard fork, knife and spoon set, decide what else is necessary based on what you serve. For example, if you serve sea food, do buy seafood forks.
- Buy durable cutlery set that lasts you longer. Stainless steel is the safest bet.
- Cutlery should be in sync with the theme of your restaurant.
- Make sure cutlery is comfortable to handle. Try it before buying.
- Buy light weight cutlery for kids.
- Have sufficient stock as a backup in case of any mishap.

While choosing the right cutlery is one of the most important things to do to make restaurants run successfully, you might also have to invest in a good software program to take care of your day-to-day operations.

Miscellaneous: Some examples of miscellaneous are: Trays, salvers, water jag, bread basket, butter dish, cruets, bud vase, menu stand,

Disposables: Disposables are extensively used in all types of catering operations, though the degree of usage is varied.

Types of F&B outlets use disposable:

Flight catering

Industrial catering

Fast food outlets

Off-premises catering

Coffee shops

Takeaway counters

Use more disposables to reduce labour and laundry costs, initial investment, and breakages. A wide range of disposables is available in different colours, sizes, qualities, and prices to suit the needs of catering operators. Disposable placemats - banquet table rolls coasters replace tablecloths. Disposable cups plates, knives, spoons, and forks substitute chinaware and cutlery. Paper napkins replace cloth napkins. Cling film is used to wrap up portioned food. Aluminum foil is used to wrap food to retain heat in takeaways

Trolley: Trollies are used in the F&B service department for serving as well as storing. Many hotels refer to a mobile service. It is also used in elite food and beverage outlets for serving the guests, from which a dish may be dressed, prepared, carved, and flambéed in the presence of guests near their table.

Type Of Trolleys

Hors d' oeuvre varies trolley

Salad trolley

Food preparation trolley

Carving trolley

Flambe trolley

Sweet trolley

Cheese trolley

Liqueur trolley

Chafing Dishes (Chafers): Chafing dishes are an essential addition to any F&b service establishment, they also come under food and beverage service equipment to keep food hot and ensure food safety. Chafing dishes are mostly used in the banquet department.

Types of chafing dishes

- Marmite Chafers
- Coffee Chafer Urns
- Standard Chafing Dishes
- Disposable Chafing Dishes
- Drop-In Chafers:
- Chafer Griddles

Types of Chafing Dishes: With so many different types and styles of chafing dishes to choose from, it can be difficult to find the right option for your business. We broke down the different chafing dish types and what they're used for to make the process simple

Standard Chafing Dishes: come in a variety of sizes and styles, but all serve the same purpose - to keep food hot. They often come with a lid that can either lift off or retract, depending on the model, and they range from economy to high-end in style.

Disposable Chafing Dishes: feature all of the warming capability of standard chafers, but they have the added benefit of being disposable, so you can save time on cleanup by throwing them away after service. These chafing dishes are ideal for outdoor parties or casual events.

Drop-In Chafers: are permanently installed into countertops or tabletops. They have an upscale presentation, and they're ideal for businesses like hotels that offer continental breakfast or buffets that are looking for a permanent chafing option.

Coffee Chafer Urns: Popular in hotels, buffets, and at catered events, coffee chafer urns are used to hold and dispense hot coffee and water for tea. These chafers are insulated to prevent heat loss, so your coffee or beverages stay hot for longer periods of time.

Marmite Chafers: A marmite chafer, also known as a soup chafer, is commonly used to keep soups, stews, sauces, gravies, hot cereals, and other liquids warm throughout your service.

Chafer Griddles: are ideal for keeping already cooked food items, such as pancakes, grilled meats, Reubens, and stir fry vegetables hot while being served. This type of chafer is open, so the smells and sounds of sizzling will help entice customers.

Chafer Sizes: Chafing dishes come in a variety of sizes, and some options are designed specifically for serving appetizers, entrees, and desserts. Here are some of the standard chafing dish sizes and their capacities to help you choose which option will meet your needs.

Full Size Chafing Dishes: Full-size dishes are typically rectangular, and they can hold between 8 and 9 quarts of food. Due to their size, full-size chafers are commonly used for holding and serving entrees, although you can use two smaller food pans and serve two types of appetizers or desserts on these dishes.

2/3 Size Chafing Dishes: Between full- and half-size chafing dishes, 2/3 size chafing dishes are usually round or square. These types of chafing dishes typically hold between 5 and 6 quarts of food, and they can be used for serving any type of food.

Half Size Chafing Dishes: One of the smallest types of chafing dishes, half-size chafing dishes are usually square or rectangular and have 4-5 quart capacities. Half-size chafing dishes are perfect for serving appetizers and side dishes.

Chafing Dishes Power Types: There are three ways that you can heat your chafer: with fuel, with electricity, or with induction. Each power type offers unique benefits that are ideal for different situations. We break down the different power types and their benefits below.

Fuel-Powered Chafing Dishes

Fuel chafers utilize fuel cans to keep the water in your chafer dish heated. There are several types of fuel that you can choose from:Gel Fuel: This type boasts strong heating performance and can last through long services.

Wick Fuel: Available in traditional and stem types, wick fuel is a safe option since the fuel cannot burn without a wick.

Eco-Friendly Fuel: There are also several kinds of eco-friendly fuel that boast the same heating power as the other types, but are made from environmentally friendly materials.

Additionally, different fuel types are made with various ingredients, allowing you even greater control over what type of chafing fuel you use.

Electric Chafing Dishes: Electric chafers are great for outdoor events as they are easier to use than chafing fuel in the event of windy or inclement weather. They're also ideal for indoor use when you don't want to deal with the hazards of open flames. Keep in mind that electric chafing dishes do require access to an electrical outlet, so plan accordingly when using them.

Induction Chafing Dishes: Induction chafers are designed for use with induction cookers or warmers to heat the unit rather than utilizing a heated water pan, like other chafing dishes. Induction cooking only heats the chafer and there is no open flame, which eliminates the hazard of burns and fires. An induction chafer also provides best-in-class heat distribution with no hot or cold spots, and they allow you to maintain a specific temperature for longer periods of time than other chafing dishes.

If you own a fuel-powered chafer but want to convert it to an electric chafer, you can use a universal electric chafer heater. Additionally, you can choose a full-size electric chafer warmer pan to replace your water pan and serve as a free-standing warming unit.

Chafing Dish Shapes: You can find chafers in several shapes, and the different shapes are used for serving different types of foods. Here are some of the common chafing dish shapes.

Rectangular Chafers: One of the most standard dish shapes, rectangular chafing dishes are commonly used for entrees. You can use these types of chafers in any type of establishment, such as hotels or banquet halls.

Round Chafers: Another popular chafing dish shape, a round chafer is commonly used for side dishes, sauces, and desserts. A variety of this type is the half-round chafer, which is typically used for appetizers and side dishes.

Oval Chafers: Oval chafers are used for serving entrees, but they have a sleek and contemporary look. As a result, they are an excellent option for establishments that want a modern alternative to rectangular chafers.

Square Chafers

Square chafers are the least common type, but they have a modern design that is complementary to contemporary aesthetics. This type is commonly used for serving appetizers and sides.

Chafing Dish Covers: Chafer covers are important for keeping your food hot and moist, but it's important to keep the crowd in mind when choosing covers. Hinged, lift-off, and roll-top lids are the most popular styles, but there are several other appealing options.

Lift Off and Dome Covers: Lift off and dome covers lift off the chafer completely, and they feature a handle on top of the lid. Most types of chafers with lift-off and dome covers have a cover holder, where customers and employees can place the cover.

Roll Top and Retractable Covers: This type of lid is ideal for buffets because customers do not need to hold the lid or even remove it. Roll-top covers generally have front handles for easy use. For two side service, choose a model that can retract on both sides. Many retractable covers have a 90-degree and 180-degree opening for versatility. Many options also feature slide locks to keep the cover in place. Keep in mind that that roll tops that don't flip down 180 degrees are only ideal for one-sided service.

Hinged Covers: Hinged covers give you the look of a lift-off unit without the hassle of having to remove the lid. Many models offer a stay-open feature at 45 and 90-degree angles. Some options even double as lift-off lids for added versatility. There are also hinged covers with slow closing hinges, which close gently and quietly, which helps preserve the atmosphere of your dining area and causes less wear and tear on the unit.

Glass Top Covers: Glass top lids feature clear windows that allow customers to view the contents without opening the lid. This helps prevents heat loss from customers opening and closing the cover regularly to see what's inside.

Regardless of the cover type you prefer, look for lids with coated handles for server safety and convenience. Covered handles are often constructed or coated with nylon to stay cool to the touch. They also provide an easy grip.

Chafing Dish Finishes: From attractive mirror finishes to subdued matte options, there are many different styles of chafers that you can choose from. Here are some popular finishes and trim styles that you can find.

Mirror Polish Finish: These chafing dishes have a shiny, reflective appearance. The finish provides a superior shine for an attractive display at any event. Although, mirror polish finishes can attract fingerprints easily, so be sure to regularly clean your chafers with a microfiber cloth. Due to their opulent finish, mirror polish chafing dishes are commonly used in fine dining settings, hotels, and at catered events.

Satin Finish: A satin finish is smooth to the touch and not reflective. It provides an upscale appearance without the shine. These options are ideal for operators that want a visually appealing design without the hassle of constantly polishing and cleaning off fingerprints.

Matte Finish: A matte finish features a surface that isn't particularly shiny or reflective. If you're looking for affordable and accessible chafing options for your buffet or hotel, these are the perfect options. The matte surface doesn't distract customers and it makes your food the focal point of your buffet line.

Hammered Copper: This finish has a dimpled texture, with the appearance of hand-hammered copper. It provides an elegant and contemporary display that is perfect for modern weddings, receptions, anniversaries, and other catered events.

Trim Styles: Chafing dishes also come in several trim styles, which add a pop of color and visual appeal to your buffet line. When choosing a trim style, keep in mind your establishment's existing decor and choose the type that best suits your concept. Here are a few common types of chafer trim styles.

Brass Trim: Brass trim adds a subtle yet sophisticated appeal to your chafer. The brass isn't as bright as gold or copper, but the dark yellow accents complement the sleek look of the silver chafing dish.

Gold Trim: Gold trim gives your chafing dish a sophisticated and elegant appeal. The gold color stands out against the chafer's silver body to create a striking presentation.

Chrome Trim: Highly polished chrome trim gives chafers a contemporary look. These options are perfect for buffets, hotels, and catering companies that are looking for chafers with a modern look.

Glassware: 12 types of glassware which includes different types of bar glasses such as cocktail glasses and tumblers, red and white whine glasses and beer glasses. Amazing diagrams for each type included. This is awesome. When choosing from the types of glassware, it's helpful to begin your intended use. Styles of glassware can point you in the right direction to what you should get. Think of the situations when you'll use them. Keep in mind who will be drinking from them too.

Everyday Usage: These are the glasses you'll use for any meal or snack. They are the low-end of the price range simply because of the risk of breaking and cost of replacement. It's not necessarily an indication of how ornate a piece is. Less expensive techniques such as etching can make a cheap one look like something for special occasions.

They include items such as short or tall tumblers you might use to pour a glass of juice or milk. They come in a variety of volumes from a few ounces to ones that'll hold an entire can of soda or more. The size may deceive you, depending on the diameter of the glass. A short, wide one can rival the volume which a taller, thinner one might contain.

Stemware: Just as the name implies, these pieces have a stem between the foot and the bowl of the glass. They can be something you use every day if you have wine with your meals. They can also be more expensive or decorative glassware that you'll use occasionally. These glasses get less use than the casual types. You'll often see some specialization with these that goes beyond size.

Design and materials play bigger roles in what you get. You may be surprised to learn that stemware plays a more important role in drinking than you may realize.

Barware: Barware falls under the same umbrella as stemware in that these are glasses with a purpose. They're often an integral part of the drinking experience. Think of a Tom Collins glass with its like cocktail name. They can range the gamut of formal, elegant pieces to silly ones to add some fun to an occasion. A close relationship exists between the typical beverage and the glass that is used.

Materials: The materials used are one factor that determines the price you'll pay for glassware. You'll see it in the design too. All of these factors will affect the user experience which we'll discuss in detail with the different types of beverage glasses.

Glass: By and large, the most common type you'll see is soda-lime glass. It's the least expensive which is reflected in its cost.

While it's cheap, it can't handle sudden changes in temperature which is why you should use only Pyrex or other heat-resistant products in your microwave. These pieces tend to be thicker because they're more fragile than other types. That also makes them dishwasher safe. This material is an excellent choice for everyday glassware because of these factors. An alternative is borosilicate glass which overcomes some of the issues of durability and heat resistance that plague the former.

Crystal: Crystal has two overwhelming advantages over glass. First, it beats the latter when it comes to a side-by-side test of which is stronger. That's because it contains lead oxide. Second, there's no denying the beauty of crystal. It simply looks stunning and makes everything in the glass look great too.

That's because of the addition of the lead which is soft and malleable. On the downside, it's expensive. And if you don't like hand washing your glassware, you're out of luck.

Non-Lead Crystal: An alternative is non-lead crystal. Rather than lead, zinc or magnesium fill in to add to its overall strength. That trait is important because you can get thinner glasses which translates into beautiful pieces. They still have the durability of regular crystal with some being dishwasher-safe too. They're an excellent option if you're looking for something more decorative.

Types of Stemware: You can think of a discussion about stemware as a launching off point into aficionado territory. We're not just talking about a wine glass, but one meant for a particular varietal. It's not just about wine either. Dessert beverages and liquors also have tapped into this specialty field. If you thought you knew it all about the types of glassware, think again.

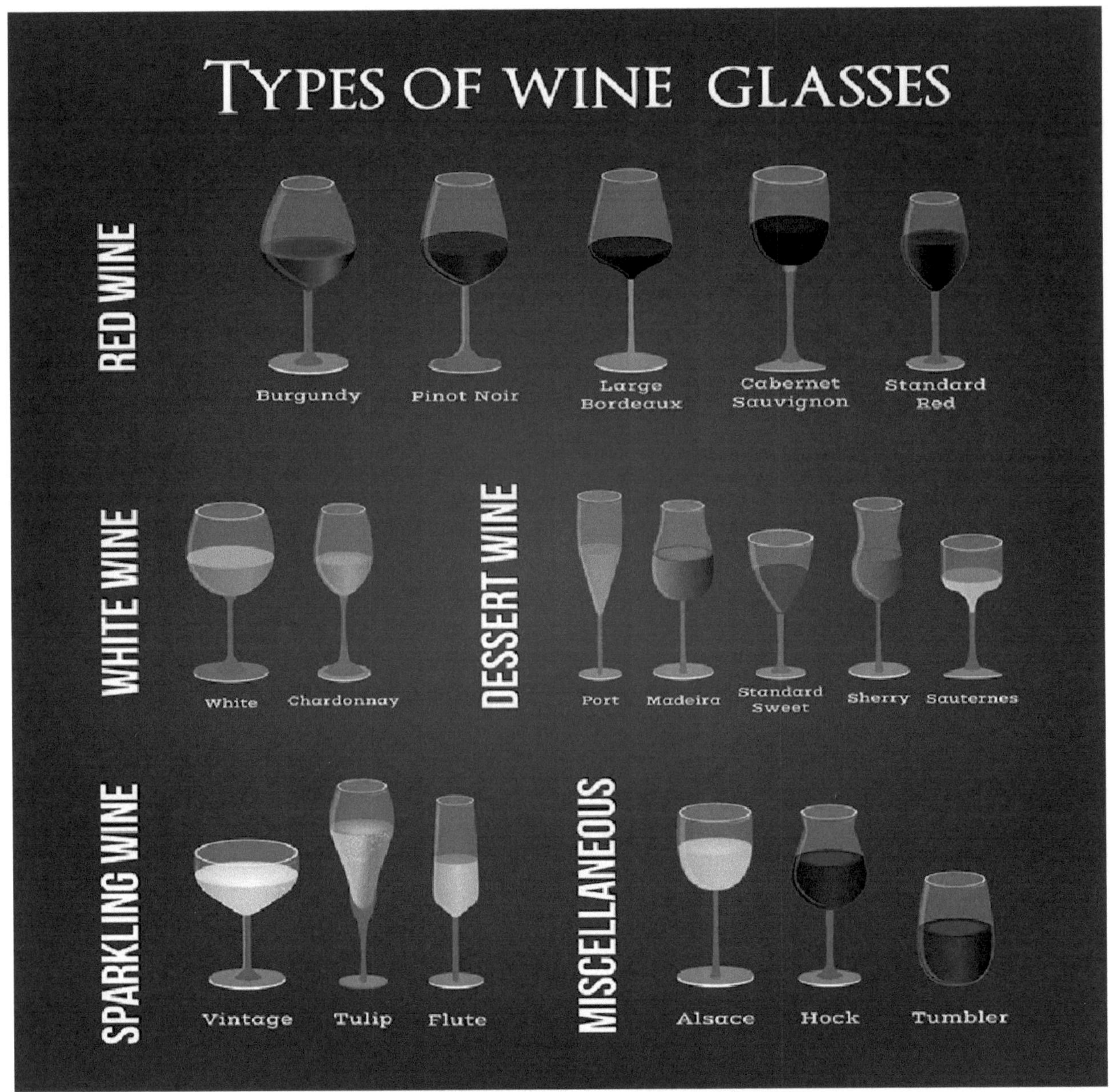

Enter Caption

Red Wine

Characterizing a wine as either red or white is just the tip of the iceberg when it comes to choosing glassware to match the beverage. There are several differences between the two main types. A red wine glass often has a larger bowl which fits in with the way it is savored and enjoyed. Often, it's desirable to decant red wine to allow for more oxygen exchange. The red wine glass reflects similar traits with a larger surface area and opening at the top. It's essential to remember that wine is a complex beverage with many layers of aromas and other traits that will

affect the experience. The design of the wine glass enhances it by minimizing other factors. But just like there are many kinds of red wine, there are several styles of glasses. You'll find ones specially made for pinot noir, Bordeaux, cabernet sauvignon along with a standard, all-purpose version. The differences rest with the varying amounts of tannins, acidity, and alcohol.

You need to experience the aromas and flavors fully to enjoy a glass of wine. That means being able to swirl it to get air to it to open it up to release volatile components. The bottom of the bowl of a red wine glass is larger than the top to direct all those wonderful smells so you can detect them better.

White Wine

White wine glasses vary in their shape and size too for similar reasons. They have a smaller bowl than a red wine glass because of their varying styles and temperature requirements. Every type of wine has its optimal serving temperature. With white wine, that generally means cold.

These beverages are often more delicate than red with aromas that are often subtle. The shape of the glass reflects these traits. You'll find wines in both light and full-bodied styles. The former tastes best with a smaller version of the all-purpose red where the shape tapers to a narrower opening. Then, of course, you have champagne glasses. You'll see several styles of these pieces as well. They include the classic coupe shape which resembles a small bowl on a stem.

There is the long and tall flute that directs the bubbles to the top slowly. One of the most popular is the tulip glass which refines the shape of the former to enhance the tasting experience.

A full-bodied white wine, on the other hand, has plenty of aromas to experience. A wine glass with straight sides and a wider opening at the top will allow you to fully experience them. Are you wondering which type you should choose? Our advice is to at least have all-purpose glasses for red and white on hand.

While Chardonnay is the most popular wine at 13.3 percent of the market, cab isn't far behind at 12.1 percent. If you prefer a certain varietal, this guide from Riedel will help you choose the best one for the wine.

Other Types: But, wait! There's more! You'll find additional types of glassware for other beverages. Again, part of it rests with the experience. The other consideration is serving size. A healthy five-ounce pour is par for the course for a red wine. It's a different story with a dessert wines and other liquors. You'll find specialty glasses for other beverages including:

Port
Sherry
Madeira
Sauternes
Scotch/Whiskey
Martini

Several factors are driving this changing market. First, people are branching out and discovering fortified wines. That has led to a desire for a better savoring experience. Second, the industry itself has grown and become more refined with new styles and techniques that are attracting another segment. Finally, a more knowledgeable consumer base has driven the demand.

Stem versus Stemless: You'll also see glassware without the stem and foot of the traditional form. On the plus side, a stemless glass is not top heavy and less likely to fall over and break.

If that is a frequent problem at your home, you might consider them as an alternative. The wine enthusiast is more likely to give them a pass. First, there are all those fingerprints. Drinking wine is a visual experience too. We can understand how it could be off-putting to some. Second, your hands will affect the temperature of the wine, sometimes, adversely. Even most red wines benefit from chilling.

Enter Caption

Our advice is to choose what works best for you and the type of wine drinking you do. What will ruin it for some won't bother others a bit. However, the other factors of design and shape still apply even if there isn't a stem on the glass. Another advantage of this type is that they're often cheaper than stemware which is worth considering.

Types of Barware:

Enter Caption

Barware tends to toe the all-purpose line simply because of the plethora of choices. You can refer back to factors such as materials to help you decide on the practical matters of aesthetics and usage. That said, you'll still see some specialization that has been market driven in some segments which are worth some discussion beginning with beer.

Beer: The beer industry has seen a tremendous amount of change in recent years. You'll see it in your choices of glassware for these beverages and their varying styles. The market as a whole hasn't moved upward a lot in recent years with growth hovering around 1 to 2 percent. The craft beer segment is the polar opposite, posting annual rates of over 13 percent.

Hefeweizens

Pour it into this specially shaped glass that locks in the aromas and enjoy your wheat that much more.

Pilsners

Get the perfect head and body distribution of pilsners and lagers in this curvaceous glass.

Ales

Get a good grip on this classic pub pint. It's perfect for IPAs, stouts and ales.

Ryes

A thinner base keeps the aromas of rye, Kölsh and bock beers locked inside so you taste every crisp, malty note.

IPAs

You'll love IPAs even more in this glass designed in partnership with Dogfish Head and Sierra Nevada.

Blondes

Perfect for delicate beers because the slender shape kicks up the malt flavor.

Stouts

Designed by Oiva Toikkain 1973, this embossed, hefty pub classic is freezer-safe for a frosty brew.

Any Craft Beer

Fit for royalty, this pint-style glass pays tribute to any well-crafted brew.

Enter Caption

There has been a surge of microbreweries, brewpubs, and regional craft breweries that are causing an incredible shift in the industry. No longer is the pilsner the only glassware for beer that you need. It also includes other types including:

Flute glasses
Goblets
Mugs
Pint glasses
Snifters
Stange
Tulip glasses
Weizen glasses

The design of each of these types is suited to a particular kind of beer. It involves things that you'll see with wine glasses but also the varying alcohol levels. Many craft beers far exceed the alcohol by volume (ABV) of under 5 percent that you find with everyday lagers. The smaller size glasses reflect this fact.

There's a lot of overlap between the types of glassware. A pint glass or a mug will cover a lot of bases. But, if you are a beer aficionado of a certain style, by all means, get the right one for what you drink. Take into account the size of the container when choosing. Craft beers, for example, often come in cans or bottles that stray far from the typical

12-ounce can.

Liquor: If you serve mixed drinks, a set of glasses that include a highball version and an on-the-rocks or old-fashioned type will do the job for most cocktails or soft drinks. We'd refer you back to materials and design to guide your choices. It's worth noting the change in serving size that has occurred with them over the years. About 20 years ago, the average serving of soda was around 6.5 ounces. Today, it reaches 20 ounces. You'll see the same thing in aperitif, wine glasses, and everyday glassware. We'll touch on the subject again when we discuss vintage pieces. Liquor glasses range from a quick pour in a shot glass to glasses to serve cordials or liqueurs

Specialty: The discussion up to now has only scratched the surface about the wide variety of glassware types available. You'll often find pieces that seem to suit just one type of beverage such as ochoko that you might use for sake or a snifter for cognac.

The design often is part of the ritual of using each one. You'll find glasses that are as iconic as the drink for which they are meant. Think of a hurricane glass for Planter's punch or other tropical drinks.

<u>Types of Glasses</u>

S.no	Name of the Glass	Size (1fl oz = 28.4 ml)	Uses
1	Cocktail glass	4-12 fl oz	Used for all kind of cocktails
2	Pony tumbler/ juice glass	4 fl oz	Used to serve all kind of juices
3	High ball glass	8-10 fl oz	Used to serve water
4	Beer mug	10-12 fl oz	Used to serve beer
5	Beer goblet	10-12 fl oz	Used to serve beer
6	Brandy balloon/snifter	8-10 fl oz	Used to serve brandy or liqueurs
7	Champagne (saucer/ flute/ tulip)	6-8 fl oz	Used to serve champagne or sparkling wine
8	Water goblet	8-10 fl oz	Used to serve water
9	Pilsner	10-14 fl oz	Used to serve the cocktail, juices, and beer
10	Sherry capita	1.75fl oz	Used to serve sherry or other sweet wine
11	Old fashion glass	8 fl oz	Used mainly to serve whiskey
12	Red wine glass	8-14 fl oz	Used to serve red wine
13	White wine glass	8-14 fl oz	Used to serve white wine
14	Tequila shot glass	1 fl oz	Used to serve tequila
15	Vodka shot glass	1 fl oz	Used to serve vodka
16	Margarita	5-6 fl oz	Used to serve cocktails

Enter Caption

Enter Caption

CHAPTER FOUR

Welcoming, seating and serving guests

First impressions can make or break a guest's experience, and the way in which you are **greeting guests** is very important as it is the first point of onsite contact. Your greeting is a way of making a Restaurant guest feel at home right away, so make sure you make it count. It's a way of starting conversation and breaking down barriers established by the unknown, and is an opportunity to connect with people that can bring about great results and create a personal bond. Some of the simplest tricks to provide the perfect welcome are to smile, attend to the guest as soon as possible, and if you're busy, recognize their presence and then go back to what you're doing until you can help them. Asking and anticipating questions that they may have will help make a guest feel comfortable and like they've made the right choice when deciding where to stay.

Your interactions with guests are important. The most important interaction, however, may be the very first: greeting your guests. Making guests feel welcome goes a long way towards making their dining experience a good one. Keep your posture and facial expressions open and welcoming. Stand up straight, look customers in the eye, and wear a friendly smile. Even if you are staffing a drive-through, it's important to smile; a positive facial expression reflects itself in the tone of your voice.

<u>Ask questions:</u>Questions are a great way to connect with guests quickly. People love to talk about themselves so giving them a chance to do so will help guests feel at home right away. Since there's typically a lot of paperwork to take care of upon arrival (well, there doesn't need to be if you're with Mews), asking questions can make the process more pleasant by **asking questions about their journey and what plans they have while they're visiting**; this way you can also capitalize on opportunities to upsell your services, tours and amenities. Asking questions is essentially a quick way to do market research and find out what your guests want.

<u>A smile goes a long way:</u>The saying goes "when I smile, the world smiles back at me." Incorporate this way of life into your welcome greeting. There's nothing better than being greeted after a long trip with a warm smile and someone asking genuinely how you are doing. A smile is also a great icebreaker.

<u>Offer to help</u>: Offering to help someone can also go a long way, even if many times your offer will be politely declined. See if they need help with their baggage or if they want to be shown around the premises. Helping your guests is a great way to go above and beyond and leave a lasting impression.

<u>Be cordial even if you're busy:</u>The hospitality industry is extremely fast-paced so it's easy to get overwhelmed by all the work you need to do. Don't let the stress get to you, and most importantly, don't let the guests see your stress. **Even if you're busy, make sure to be cordial to the guests** and let them know you're busy and that you'll try to be with them as quickly as possible. In this way they will feel reassured and not mind the wait.

<u>Make guests feel special:</u>There's always enough time to make your guests feel special. Consult the booking to find out if there's a birthday or special occasion they are celebrating. If so, acknowledge the special occasion upon check-in. This will go a long way. If you want to go even further, why not have a bottle of champagne or flowers in their room to greet them?

Acknowledge and Welcome Guest

- To make guest feel welcome and important, whenever any guest arrives, it is the responsibility of the service staff to approach and meet the guest with a smile, maintain eye contact and with proper body posture greet the accordingly at the door.

- As discussed before, the first employee who gets contact with customer, has the opportunity to make a positive impression on guest. In fine dining, guests are generally welcomed by hosts or hostess or may be even by the owner but in normal cases, a server or waiter or waitress may be the first person who acknowledge and welcome guest; Each and every employee should have the training to greet guest.
- The employee who greets the guest should use very brief but welcoming phrase to greet guest like "Good Morning/Afternoon/ Evening, Sir/Madam Welcome to XYZ(Name of Your Restaurant). Must remember ladies should be greeted first. In some restaurants, guests can leave their belongings like umbrella or overcoat in the reception. If you have such arrangement then politely ask guest about it.

Check Guest Reservation

- Check reservation and ask about any special need
- To be ensured whether guests have any reservation or booking very politely ask "Do you have any reservation?"
- If the answer is Yes which means guests have reservation, then thank for guests' name by saying May I have your name please" . Check your reservation book and repeat the reservation back to guest.
- If there is one guest who comes without reservation then instead of saying "Are you alone, Sir/ Madam" you could ask "Table for one person?"
- If you have enough free table then ask (if appropriate): "Do you have any preference sir like ,sitting in a smoking or non-smoking area or near the window etc.
- Ask about special need. For example there is a child in the group then ask guest whether the baby needs any high chair or not.

Handle Difficult Situations

- Example :-A guest or group of guests may come without any reservation. In that case, greeter or host could say "Please allow me few seconds sir. Let me check if there is any table available or not."
- Now if there is free table then the host could easily make guest seated there but what does happen if every tables are occupied? If none available then you have to handle the situation tactfully.

If you have bar facilities or if your restaurant is in a hotel then you may say
"Sir, I am very sorry. All the tables are occupied. Would you mind wait in our bar or in the lobby so that I can call you as soon as any of the table is free. In such way, you just prevent your restaurant from losing a very potential guest and also promoting the revenue of bar or any other business.

How to Arrange Seating Capacities

- Allocate table according to the number of guests or size of the party. For a group or large family, seat guests in a large round table or if appropriate join 2 tables together and for couple, seat in a deuce. Deuce is a hotel or restaurant term which means a table with 2 sitting space.
- Young couples trend to choose corner or near window to have romantic moment. Elderly or disabled guests should be seated near entrance so that he or she would not need to walk much. Loud, noisy parties could be arranged in private rooms or at least in the back so that other guest don't feel discomfort.
- Above all, if guests wish to get seated in particular areas and if situation permits then try your best to offer that.

Lead Guest To The Table

- Maintain eye contact throughout, keep smiling and escort the guest to the table by saying "This way please Mr./Mrs. or Sir/Madam
- Show the way by walking in front of the guest

- Do not walk too fast. Maintain very small distant, not more than one meter away from guest and look back at the guest rapidly.
- While you would reach the table, say: “Will this table be all right for you, Mr./Mrs./Ms or Sir/ Madam”

Help The Guest While Seating

- In a courteous manner pull the chair out so that there would be just enough space for the guest to enter.
- Lady Guest should be seated first with best view of the restaurant, then the gentleman.
- While helping lady guest to be seated (if applicable) stand behind the chair, push with two hands on the chair shoulder and keep the right toe at the base of the chair so that guest can seat comfortably.
- Help the kid to get into pull high chairs.

Before Leaving The Table

- At this stage the hostess or host or greeter should leave the table at this stage and return to the reception desk to welcome and continue seating procedure for other guests.
- Server may be busy in other table. Before leaving the table host or greeter should let the guest know that server has been, informed and will come very shortly.
- A very good gesture from a server should be come to the table and say "I am very sorry Sir, We are very busy at the moment.I will be with you in XYZ (required waiting time)
- Prior to leaving the table, wish the guest (by name)
- At this stage, a service staff like waiter or server will take over the table to complete next steps.
- Be friendly but very polite and courteous all the time.
- Always speak with a clear and confident tone.
- Keep smiling throughout so that guest feel comfortable.
- Guest with reservation should always be given more preference than walk-in guests.

CHAPTER FIVE

Proper table setting, food delivery and tray/ glass holding techniques

The style of table setting you choose for your dining room or catered events sends a message to your guests, letting them know what type of service they can expect to receive. An empty table with no place setting is a clear indicator that the service will be casual. By simply adding a set of silverware or place mat, you can elevate the dining experience. Usually, the more items used in a table setting, the more formal the service.

Table settings are also useful for establishing the tone at wedding receptions, banquets, and events. Caterers and wedding coordinators can use different styles of wedding table settings to indicate whether the event is formal or casual. Setting a table for your guests shows attention to detail and an indication that you care about their needs. Read on if you're interested in learning more about the different types of table settings.

How to set a restaurant table : There are lots of things to consider when learning how to set a table in a restaurant. Here is what we will be covering:

- **Table Mats**
- **Napkins**
- **Plates**
- **Cutlery**
- **Glasses**
- **Centre pieces**

Some restaurants like to have their own variations on how they set their tables, but here is the standard process.

Table Mats: Before placing down any mats, make sure they are all clean and wiped down. Be sure there is no food markings or dust on them. Table mats should be positioned straight and parallel to the edge of the table. Each diner should have plenty of space to move around.

Napkins: Normally, napkins are folded into a triangle. A standard size napkin (a small folded square) can be folded in half to achieve the triangle shape while a larger size napkin may need to be folded in half and then folded again. Make sure the napkin is neatly folded, if it looks scrunched and creased it will look untidy.

The folded napkin is then placed on the right side of the table mat. Some restaurants prefer to place the napkin in a wine glass.

Plates: Plates should be placed in the middle of the table mat and the cutlery set around it. If you are setting a small bread plate, it will be placed on the top left of the table mat.

The small bread knife is placed flat on the bread knife, parallel to the edge of the table.

Cutlery: Most restaurants prefer to offer two sets of cutlery for guests (starter and main course), then provide cutlery for dessert if the customer decides to order something sweet. The dinner knife and fork are placed parallel on either side of the table mat (forks on the left, knives on the right). Then the smaller knife and fork for the starter are placed on the outside of the dinner cutlery.

If you want to set the dessert cutlery down too, the dessert fork and spoon are placed at the top of the table mat. They lie parallel to the mat, the fork lies closest with the top facing right and the spoon lies above the fork, facing left.

Glasses: Wine glasses are set on the right-hand side of the place mat. The white wine glass is placed above the main course knife, the red wine glass and water glass are placed behind it to form a triangular shape. Ensure all glasses are clean and polished before being placed. Seeing fingerprints on a wine glass is unappealing.

Centre pieces: Centre pieces are a great way to add a little extra care and attention to your table. They are usually placed at the center of the table. A small vase of flowers is a popular choice for center pieces. Make sure the flowers are healthy and replace when necessary.

Types of Table Settings: The three most common types of table settings are formal, casual, and basic. Each place setting includes the utensils and dinnerware pieces that would normally be used with the corresponding style of dining. For instance, a formal table setting will provide more utensils because there are more courses. A basic table setting provides fewer utensils because there is one course. Only provide the types of flatware or glassware that will be used during the meal. If there is no wine being served, you can remove the wine glasses. Make sure to choose the right tableware for your settings. Formal settings should be set with elegant, high-quality pieces while practical, economical tableware is more suited for basic settings.

Rule: A general rule for silverware placement is that utensils are placed in the order they are used, from the outside in. For example, the salad fork will be used before the dinner fork, so it should be placed on the outside. Forks always go on the left side of the plate, and knives and spoons are always placed on the right side. If you're providing a dessert spoon and dessert fork, they are placed above the plate.

Formal Table Setting: This is the style of place setting you will see used at fine dining restaurants, formal events, and black tie weddings. Designed for a six course meal including an appetizer, soup, salad, a starch, a protein, and dessert, this setting employs more flatware and glassware than the other settings.

Charger plates can also be used and should be placed beneath the serving plate.

Enter Caption

Follow these steps to create a formal dinner table setting:

1. Begin by placing an ironed tablecloth on the table.
2. A serving plate goes in the center of the place setting.
3. A bread plate should be placed to the top left of the serving plate. Place a butter knife on top of the bread plate with the blade facing down, and the handle towards the right.
4. Silverware on the left side of the serving plate begins with the salad fork on the outside, and the dinner fork on the inside.
5. Silverware on the right side of the serving plate, from the inside out, will consist of a dinner knife, salad knife, soup spoon, and tea spoon.
6. All flatware should be evenly spaced, and the bottoms should line up with the bottom of the serving plate.
7. The dessert spoon should be placed directly above the serving plate, in horizontal alignment with the handle towards the right.
8. Place a water glass above the dinner knife.

9. Place the white wine glass below the water glass and slightly to the right.
10. Place the red wine glass above the white wine glass and slightly to the right.
11. A cup and saucer should be placed above the soup spoon and slightly to the right.

Casual Table Setting: Commonly used at banquets and luncheons, this setting is also referred to as an informal table setting. It's a popular choice for wedding table settings and contemporary casual restaurants that want to elevate their dining room decor.

This setting is similar to a formal table setting, but is designed for three courses instead of six. The flatware provided will be enough for a soup or salad, main course, and dessert.

Enter Caption

Follow these steps to create a casual table setting:

1. A serving plate should be placed in the middle of the table setting.

2. A bread plate should be placed to the top left of the serving plate. Place a butter knife on top of the bread plate with the blade facing down, and the handle towards the right.
3. Silverware on the left side of the serving plate begins with the salad fork on the outside, and the dinner fork on the inside.
4. Silverware on the right side of the serving plate, from the inside out, will consist of a dinner knife, soup spoon, and tea spoon.
5. Place a water glass above the dinner knife.
6. Place the wine glass to the right of the water glass.

Basic Table Setting: This simple table setting is appropriate for all types of restaurants and casual events. You'll commonly see it used in diners and family restaurants along with a placemat or a coffee cup. Using a basic table setting makes your guests feel welcome and ensures they have the utensils they need.

Enter Caption

Follow these steps to create a basic table setting:

1. A serving plate should be placed in the middle of the table setting.
2. A napkin is placed to the left of the plate.
3. The fork rests on top of the napkin.
4. A knife is placed to the right of the plate.
5. A water glass or coffee cup is optional, placed above the knife and slightly to the right.

Once you have an understanding of the traditional table setting, you can add your own personal touches. Many restaurants choose not to use place settings and place wrapped silverware at each seat instead. While this is convenient, it doesn't have the same visual effect as a beautifully set table. It's up to you to decide what type of experience you want to create for your guests.

Table Setting for Buffet Service

Since there are almost limitless options as to how to set up the buffet table at catered events, hotel dining rooms and restaurants, we have compiled a short list of suggestions to help the buffet style service run more smoothly and efficiently, while leaving the creativity up to you.

- If there is enough space, set the napkin and silverware on the guest tables. An attractive folded napkin and shiny flatware make the tables look elegant and inviting.

  At buffet tables, the informal table setting is the most widely accepted format.

- Try to set the guest tables to hold everything your guests need, except for their actual dinner plates. This makes the table look attractive and it also makes it much more functional.
- It's a good idea to set up one or two condiment tables away from the main buffet as this will shorten wait time for guests at the main buffet.
- If possible, place the condiments, including salt and pepper, butter, sour cream, dressings, and more on the guest tables. This means a greater investment in owning more condiment servers, but it may be well worth your while to have satisfied customers. Sometimes it is the little conveniences that can keep guests happy without a great financial outlay on your part.

General Table Setting Checklist

- Do not include any more than three utensils on either side of the dinner plate at a time, except when an oyster (or seafood) fork is being used in addition to the other three forks.
- Dessert spoons and forks should be brought in on the dessert plate just before dessert is served.
- Everything should be geometrically spaced with every item at equal distances and all the utensils balanced.
- Make sure there is ample room between place settings.
- Before your guests are seated, the butter should be waiting on butter plates, the glasses filled with water, and the wine ready to be served.
- Place knives with blades facing the plate.

Napkin Folding: Today, there are large varieties of napkins available in different colors and materials. Paper napkins are used majorly for informal dining whereas for formal dining, linen napkins are preferred. Napkin can be folded in a number of attractive ways. They can be shaped as a flower, a character, or some object. A well-folded and well-placed napkin on the plate grabs the attention of the guests.

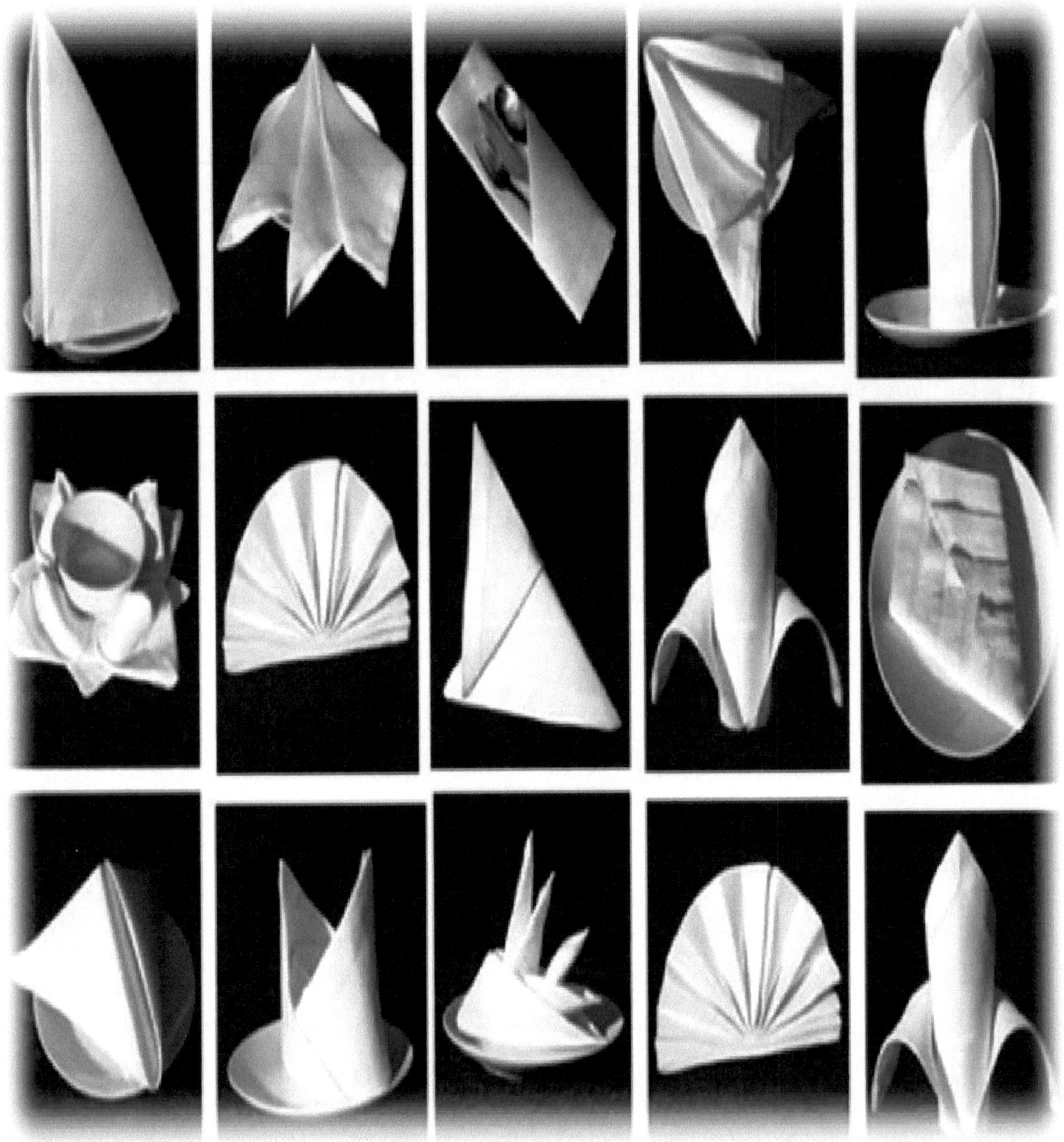

Enter Caption

Food Presentation: Presentation of a food or beverage is equally important as its recipe as the other senses are stimulated through sight and aroma. A well-prepared dish is complete only when it is presented with beautiful garnish in an appropriate food container or platter. The serving staff must follow the basic guidelines for food presentation –

- It must be presented at the required temperature.
- It must be presented according to the serving size.
- It must be presented in appropriate hollowware of suitable size.

- It is also recommended to serve food with the right garnish that adds to the catchiness of the dish. The garnish in contrast color is quite appealing.
- The garnish or accompaniment should not overshadow the main food.

The cook needs to be creative at presenting the dish so well that the final result comes out as a treat for not only the taste buds but also for the eyes.

Beverage Presentation: Beverage presentation gains a lot of importance in today's world. Beverages taste good if they are presented at the temperature at which they are meant to have. Right from selecting the appropriate service glassware, creating various pleasant color schemes of the ingredients, and serving the beverage with creative ideas pays.

For example, the coconut water from a tender coconut can be served in the neatly cut and clean tender coconut itself from which it is taken out. Also, mocktails or cocktails can be presented with straws and slices of fruits in different shapes and colors.

CHAPTER SIX

Understanding Point of Sale systems

Point-of-sale information is information that is gathered from your daily (or even hourly) receipts. Before computerized equipment was available, a supervisor would analyze the sales at the end of each day using the handwritten guest cheques. The total number of customers, the average cheque size, and the amounts of each entrée sold were tallied and recorded. The supervisor would also compute total sales, check cash against cash register totals, and complete other financial records. The information from the sales analysis was used by the chef or restaurant manager to manage inventory, predict volume of sales, and judge the popularity of items. The high volume of cash and credit cards that pass through a restaurant each day make a POS system a necessity. Not only does a POS system track every penny of your sales, many POS programs also act as credit card processors. This makes swiping credit cards more secure for both the customer and the business. Servers are accountable for all their sales, and it is impossible to alter checks in the computer unless you have the password. This helps cut down on employee theft.

Benefits: One benefit of a POS system is that it simplifies communications between the kitchen and the wait staff. Orders go through the computer, directly to the kitchen printer. Another benefit of a restaurant POS program is that it can track everything from food usage to the most popular menu items. Because the POS system acts as a time clock, it can also help prepare payroll. This can save you a lot of money in your bookkeeping department. Along with the daily operations of running a restaurant, a POS system can organize profit and loss statement and sales tax.

Drawbacks: The most obvious drawback to any POS system is that it is a computer, and subject to all the same technological whims. If it happens to crash and you don't have a backup, then you risk losing all your data, not just sales, but profit and loss statements and payroll statements. Important stuff that the IRS may want to examine some day. So, always have a backup.

Types of Point-of-Sale Equipment

Today, most point-of-sales reports are generated automatically by point-of-sales (POS) hardware and software. A simple POS system may be a single cash register connected to a computer terminal that stores data, or it may be more complex with multiple terminals, handheld devices or tablets, and even smartphones connected to the system by supported applications, and also connected to printers at various points in the

system that will print orders directly in the kitchen or bar area. Allow you to maintain efficient customer service in your restaurant without compromising your quality of service is great for the bottom line of a family entertainment center or restaurant.

POS systems consist of a number of terminals connected to a central processing unit. For a terminal to process transactions, it must be connected to the central unit which houses the software and memory to process the information. Several types of terminals may be available. A pre-check terminal is used to enter orders; it has no cash drawer.

Many pre-check terminals are now available in hand-held cordless models, or tablets or smartphones can be used for this purpose. In some systems, a pre-check terminal is used to enter and print the orders for a table. The printed copy is then given to the kitchen to relay the order. In other systems, the order is sent directly from the pre-check machine to a printer in the kitchen or bar. The server does not have to carry the order over to the pickup counter.

A separate cashier terminal is used to settle guests' cheques. The information may also be sent automatically to a journal printer and a manager workstation. The journal printer is usually located in a secure area and provides management with a detailed systems audit.

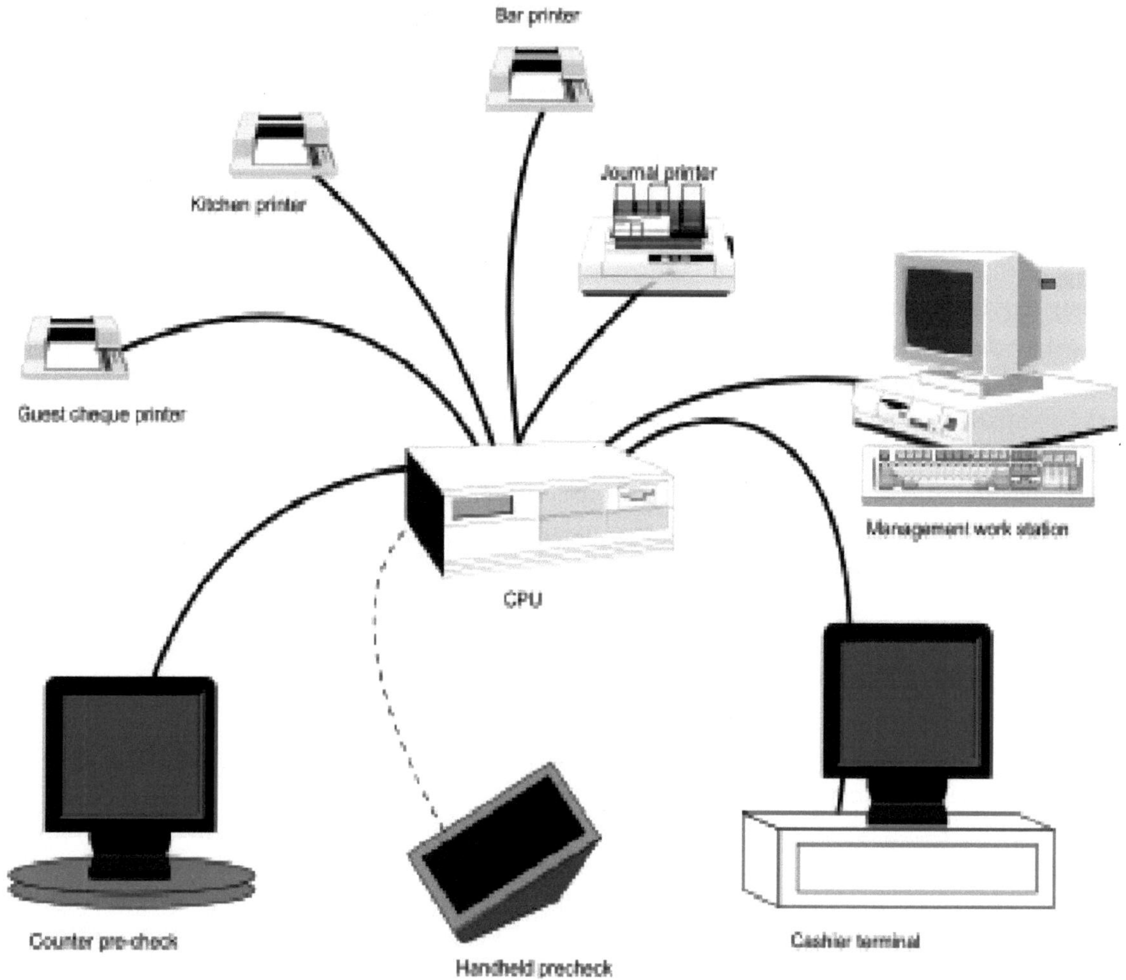

Enter Caption

POS information is a powerful tool that permits you to analyze menu performance and revise menus, forecast labour requirements, forecast inventory requirements, and analyze staff performance and sales. POS systems have the ability to generate

- Sales analysis reports
- Labour reports such as employee hours, wages, credits for meals, numbers of guests served per server, gross sales per server, average cheque size per server, and so forth
- Inventory files that can be used by inventory management software to automatically deduct items from inventory based on the standard recipe for a menu item
- Other management reports such as a daily revenue report

Sales Analysis Report: A sales analysis report analyzes sales by menu item. It can be computed for any period of time including an hour, a meal period (e.g., breakfast, lunch), a day, a week, or a month. The detailed reporting permits you to identify peak periods precisely. Fast-food restaurants will often want to analyze sales hourly to maximize the utilization of labour. The report includes:

- Number of items sold in each period
- Individual and total food cost for each menu item during the period (based on standard recipes and standard costs)
- Total food cost for the period (also called expected cost or ideal cost)
- Ideal food cost percentage

Ideal Food Cost: The ideal food cost is based on actual items sold. It is calculated by multiplying the actual number of items sold by the standard food cost per item, then summing the costs for all menu items. The ideal food cost is then compared to actual food costs. The standard recipe and standard cost must be regularly updated and recalculated for the comparison to be valid. The two costs should be fairly close. Minor variations can be the result of special purchases of bulk items or the use of small quantities of some items that are not restocked on a weekly basis. Larger discrepancies may indicate waste due to spills and spoilage, pilferage, poor portion control, changes in quality and yield of stock (e.g., due to overcooking). Customer complaints can result in an item being discarded without being charged or a second item being cooked.

Menu Analysis and Engineering: Sales analysis reports provide detailed information that can be very helpful in menu planning. The reports can analyze the profitability and popularity of each item. You can then use the results to review the menu and make changes. Refer to the section of this book on menu engineering for more detail on how to use this information.

SaveTime: The a key benefit of a entertainment POS or fun center POS system is the significant increase in efficiency of taking and relaying orders to the kitchen or bar.

Waiters have continuous mobility around the restaurant, while clearly communicating and recording orders. This gives the customers the convenience of table side ordering, whilst also allowing the orders to recorded and distributed seamlessly. This means that customers will be served, receive their meals and leave quickly, without any loss in the overall quality of the experience, relative to what they would've had prior to the entertainment POS or fun center POS system.

TheftControl: Theft control may not seem like a particularly pressing issue, especially if your products are behind the counter and require customers to order and pay for them before accessing them.

Regardless, an entertainment POS or fun center POS system will make you aware of any potential issues of theft through tracking what is ordered and what is paid for. Another area which an entertainment POS or fun center POS system can assist you in saving money is through regulating how much of each individual inventory item is used for products you serve.

This relates specifically to those businesses that serve food and beverage which isn't pre-made. It is important to have set measures for staff to follow in recipes, which allows you to see how much inventory is actually left compared to how much should be left based on the inventory management system.

BuildsCustomerRelationships: An entertainment POS or fun center POS system can obviously help your business in many different ways, from recording sales to keeping track of inventory levels. However, it can also be utilized in the building of customer relationships. Collecting customer details, namely an email address, will mean that you can communicate with past customers after their visit.

This makes it easy to them send discounts, gift cards or other rewards to incentivize past customers to return. If you have a loyalty program you will also be able to use a entertainment POS or fun center POS system to enhance its effectiveness. This can be done by tracking customer order history, identifying what their favorite food and beverages are and customizing special discounts and offers accordingly. Furthermore, you can run schemes in loyalty programs where customers can receive discounts and based on how much they spend or other variations of this.

Forecasting Inventory Requirements: POS information can also be used to forecast inventory and staff requirements. If you have sales records that indicate that in a typical week you sell 84 portions of fish and 97 portions of tikka chicken, you can look at your current inventory and decide how much you need to order for the coming week.

Manage Staff: POS information can also be used to manage staff. The software will allow you to prepare reports that track the sales of each server. You might be able to determine the average cheque size of guests served by each server. You could also track the amount of alcohol, appetizer, and dessert sales to see whether your servers are suggestively selling these items. If you have an incentive program to sell specific menu items or specials, you could track the staff member's performance. These reports may be used to give feedback to staff on their performance and suggest methods of improving their sales.

How a POS Can Simplify Managing Your Restaurant

Managing an entertainment business requires a great deal of organization throughout all levels of the business. POS systems offer a great range of benefits aiding in the simplification of many business processes, from inventory management to staff management.

Employees are essentially the backbone of entertainment and food and beverage based businesses, without them the business fails to run. As a result, employee management is a highly important task, however an entertainment POS or fun center POS system can help streamline the process. Clearly managing time clocks, scheduling which employees work each shift, keeping payroll up to date are all tasks entertainment POS or fun center POS can potentially assist with.

Overall, the POS system has become a very effective tool for the industry to collect and manage a wide array of information. The advantages that the technology has brought are in the rapid calculation and analysis of a large amount of data, but all of these systems still require those who operate them and interpret the data to have a solid understanding of the principles of effective kitchen management and cost controls.

CHAPTER SEVEN

Strategies for creating a memorable customer experience

Does your Restaurant deliver an amazing customer experience every time? If you hesitated with your answer, it might be time to make some adjustments. A great customer experience can be inexpensive to deliver and can generate rewards for years to come. We put together a list of the top things construction companies can do to create a memorable experience for their customers. Satisfaction plays an important role: 60% of guests finding themselves "very satisfied" go on to recommend their hotel. Yet, one category of guests is intriguing, as their recommendation rates can reach 97%! These are guests who claim to have experienced a "pleasant surprise" during their visit. In terms of customer engagement, having an exceptional moment is thus of greater impact than having an overall positive experience. This assessment is of paramount importance at a time when more and more companies are looking to distinguish themselves through client experience or employee experience. It tells us two things: first, a satisfactory experience is not necessarily a memorable one. In the first instance, the company strives to avoid any mishap or disagreement. It aims for the perfect experience, running the risk of making it too sleek for the person living it. In contrast, memorable experiences are indeed pleasant but moreover, they are lit with a few remarkable moments—surprises for example—that really make a lasting impression.

The second lesson is that focusing on creating remarkable moments is an investment with a strong likelihood of reward. Customers who experience such moments are more attached emotionally to the brand that provided it, and are more inclined to recommend it. The same is true with staff. John Deere, for example, has carefully planned its inception program for new staff, making this a distinctive aspect of its employer brand. The group has since noticed a greater level of involvement among its employees and an increase in its appeal factor.

Talk it out: Whether it's an estimate or an email, be clear with your customers. Don't assume anything and encourage them to ask any question. Nothing is more frustrating than feeling like someone is talking down to you, so take your time to explain procedures, timelines and budgets in the least complicated way possible. If your customers feel they are respected, they'll show you the same courtesy.

Be available, even when you aren't: When a customer or prospective customer reaches out to you, be prompt in your reply or they may take their business elsewhere. Make sure you are easy to reach by using multiple forms of communication — phone calls, email, social media or your website. Always be clear about your availability.

If you don't take calls after a certain time of day, is there someone else on the team they can contact, or should they send an email? It's important that your website is up-to-date with correct contact information and business hours. Every customer should feel like they are a priority to you.

If you're not early, you're late: Whether you've scheduled an in-person meeting or a phone call, be punctual. Make sure you are on time and available for your customer when they need something. If a delivery is delayed or a deadline can't be met, be sure to **communicate in advance**. Forgiveness for little hiccups is easy when they are communicated early!

Harness the power of your team: Make sure your team is well-versed when it comes to your customer service expectations. Take the time to train them on best practices for delivering the optimal customer experience. Give your team boundaries so they know how far their personal authority extends and when it's time to bring you in to problem solve.

Technology is not optional: Streamline and enhance your customers' experiences through technology. A modern, user-friendly website can also serve many purposes. It's your company's online home and creates a first impression that demonstrates your expertise and reliability. Social media can inspire and educate your customers and prospective customers, too!

Meet your customers where they are: Know your customer and have a clear understanding of their budget. Work within their budget and avoid any hidden costs that result from unclear or incorrect estimates. Set reasonable expectations about what you can and cannot do within their budget, along with a realistic timeline for the work.

Fix errors fast: If a mistake is made, acknowledge your customer's concerns as soon as possible and accept responsibility if there is an error on your part. Take the time to correct any issues the first time. It is important to offer guarantees on your work.

Focus on relationships: you must work at building trust and fostering a relationship with your customers. If they trust you, they will be more likely to spread the word to others and help you build your business, as well as help you foster a trusted reputation within the community.

When a construction project is complete and a customer is satisfied, take the time to send an email and show them your appreciation. It is much more likely that they will do business with you in the future if you work at building a rapport with them. And, they might even feel compelled to write an online review for you!

Under promise and over deliver: Customers always remember positive surprises, and they never forget negative ones. I'm still impressed when a package arrives a day earlier than promised or I get a free promotion with my order. Pleasant surprises don't have to be big -- like how fast you return a phone call or email.

Experience is made up of three different factors:

Basic factors: These factors are expected and taken for granted. They do not lead to satisfaction when they are delivered, but if they are missing they will cause dissatisfaction. A good example can be a clean hotel room. You most likely won´t brag about it to your friends, but if the room is dirty it will likely be your first complaint.

Performance factors: These experiences will make you unsatisfied if they're not fulfilled, and will for sure make you more satisfied if they are delivered. A good example is the experience you get from a warm and welcoming staff in the hotel. While an uninterested, rude or abrupt staff will leave you unsatisfied, disappointed or maybe even angry.

Excitement or delight factors: These factors are unexpected and when they happen they will surprise us and delight us. The x-factor. When they are missing they will not be noticed, but these are the type of factors that make the experience a whole lot better, and it can make the experience unforgettable. Once more we can use the hotel as example. Let's say the staff share their local secrets with you, or have a personalized gift ready for you in your room, chances are you will be delightfully surprised. One common way to think about experiences is to divide it across two dimensions. The first dimension corresponds with customer participation. This means tourists can be an active or a passive part of the experience. The second dimension describes the connection or physical relationship that connects customers with the experience. The range can be from absorption to immersion. Whether an experience is memorable or not depends on what happens when the visitor interacts with a destination or site. It also depends on co-creation. This means that the clients create their own experiences, in the unique context of each contact point, between them and the host.

The creation of value happens when these guests are enabled to personalize their experience, using the stage your business or destination set up.

Impact on Loyalty: The core purpose of this is to build customer loyalty. It's therefore important to understand the relative impact the different memorable events are likely to have on customers' future behaviour. The simplest way to explain this is to imagine that each customer has a 'loyalty account'; an account of the 'feelings' they have towards their suppliers and how those feeling will influence their future behaviour. Like a bank account, it could be in credit or debit; the more in credit the more loyal that customer will be, the more in debit the more disloyal. And like a bank account it will receive deposits and withdrawals based on the experiences the customer has with the supplier.

The various customer experiences explained above would have the following relative affect on the loyalty account.

- Positive Experiences – Lets say that every positive experience, whether it be during a First Impression, a Significant Event or a Last Impression, will increase the loyalty account by +1 – a one-element increase in loyalty.
- Negative Experiences – Using the same scale, then every negative experience will decrease the loyalty account by -3 – a three-element decrease in loyalty. This means that each negative experience will need three positive experiences simply to neutralise its negative impact on loyalty.
- Recovery Experiences – Again using the same scale, every recovery experience will increase the loyalty account by +6 – a six-element increase in loyalty. So this is the most powerful loyalty builder and should be used at every opportunity.

The key is to remember that the expectation, experience and the memory of it need managing. And with a little care and attention it's possible (and easy) to ensure that expectation and experience management will influence current behaviour and spend and memory management will influence future behaviour and loyalty. So perhaps it's time for another switch in focus, from Customer Experience Management to Customer Expectation, Experience and Memory Management?

CHAPTER EIGHT

Strategies for managing difficult interactions with guests.

The customer is always right," they may not always be easy to deal with. Learning how to deal with difficult customers is an important step for any business manager, especially those who work in the Hospitality service industry. Even businesses with the best products and services are bound to have occasional run-ins with angry customers. To build a positive reputation with consumers, it is important to have properly trained staff who can handle difficult people and resolve customer complaints.

Our natural response is to get defensive and get into a negative mindset with a disgruntled client. Once you flip the switch and start with 'thank you,' the response is out of the ordinary for them. This works in every business, and once the strategy is taught to the customer service teams, sales divisions, and leadership, the impact is amazing. However, handling an angry customer doesn't stop there. Here are several other techniques and strategies that your team can learn to enhance the quality of customer service when dealing with complaints.

Difficult customer experience scenarios

The impatient customer

The situation: An impatient customer may have been waiting in line longer than usual, they may be running late to their next appointment, or maybe they're restless while you search for a solution to their issue or concern.

How to handle it: Be clear and to the point without appearing dismissive of their demeanor. Explain transparently why there's a wait or delay without getting into specifics. Make sure an impatient customer knows that effort is being invested in resolving the situation.

Frame your answers in a positive light, too. For example, instead of saying that an item is out of stock, explain that a preparation delivery is expected delay by 30 minutes because of technical glitch or that you are working quickly to sort out technical glitch.

The indecisive customer

The situation: An indecisive customer struggles to choose between several products or service options, but they may not communicate this concern to you.

How to handle it: Ask specific questions about some of the most common factors that impact decision-making, including features, service tiers and price. If you have any literature that can help them make a decision, point them to those resources as well. Most importantly, listen to their concerns with care.

The angry customer

The situation: No matter the scenario or solution, an angry customer is simply not satisfied with the end result, and attempts to rectify the situation are not helping or are worsening the situation.

How to handle it: Even if you don't feel it's warranted, begin the interaction by apologizing for the issue. Try to resolve the situation by addressing pointed grievances they have regarding the subject at hand. Remember to keep it brief: The longer you linger, the more opportunities for grievances arise and the less time you have to spend with your other customers.

The demanding customer

The situation: A demanding customer zaps lots of your energy and time, often at the expense of other customers. They may be dead set on the product or solution they want and may not accept alternatives, even those that are a better fit for their needs.

How to handle it: Speak slowly and be patient. Hear their concerns and move swiftly to address them. Be transparent, too; answers to buy time or put off their needs while addressing other customers may not go over well.

The vague customer

The situation: This customer comes to your restaurant without a clear idea of what they need. They may have difficulty articulating the problem, or they may not have a complete understanding of their options. As you ask questions to get to the heart of the issue, the answers don't necessarily help or may even add more confusion to the situation.

How to handle it: Just like with the indecisive customer, ask a vague customer pointed and specific questions about their needs. This is more likely to provide the information you need to best help them.

Each question you ask should be with the purpose of getting to the bottom of the situation so you don't spend too much time while other customers are waiting.

The customer that demands a refund

The scenario: This customer type is so disappointed or unhappy with the product or service that they are requesting their money back.

How to handle it: Each company has their own refund policy, as well as regulations that determine what items can be taken back. While the best course of action is to provide a refund in full or in part, your company may want to offer a credit toward future purchases.

If you do give the refund, be clear about when it was processed and how long they can expect it to take.

The unhappy customer

The situation: Despite your best efforts to resolve their situation, the customer is still dissatisfied with the resolutions offered.

How to handle it: An angry customer and an unhappy customer require a similar response. Begin with an apology, even if you don't feel like one is warranted. Briefly take stock of the solutions offered and attempt to offer something else; consult your company policies to determine what you can offer in this situation. During the conversation, don't dismiss their concerns or complaints; listen with a sympathetic and attentive ear.

Dealing with difficult customers

- **First and foremost, listen:** Do not try to talk over the customer or argue with them. Let the customer have their say, even if you know what they are going to say next, that they don't have all the information or that they are mistaken. As you listen, take the opportunity to build rapport with the customer.
- **Build rapport through empathy:** Put yourself in the customer's shoes. Echo the source of their frustration and show that you understand their position and situation. If you can empathize with a customer's problem, it will help calm them down.
- **Lower your voice:** If the customer gets louder, speak slowly, in a low tone. Your calm demeanor can carry over to them and help them to settle down.

As you approach the situation with a calm, clear mind, unaffected by the customer's tone or volume, their anger will generally dissipate.

- **Respond as if all your customers are watching:** Pretend you are not talking only to the customer but to an audience that is watching the interaction. This shift in perspective can provide an emotional buffer if the customer is being verbally abusive and will allow you to think more clearly when responding. Since an unruly customer can be a negative referral, assume they'll repeat the conversation to other potential customers; this mindset can help you do your best to address their concerns in a calming way.
- **Know when to give in:** If it is apparent that satisfying a rude customer is going to take two hours and a bottle of aspirin and still result in negative referrals, it may be better to take the high road and compromise in their favor.

This will give you more time to nurture other, more productive customer relationships. Keep in mind that the interaction is atypical of customers and you're dealing with an exception.

- **Stay calm:** If the customer is swearing or being verbally abusive, take a deep breath and continue as if you didn't hear them. Responding in kind will not solve anything, and it will usually escalate the situation. Instead, remind the customer that you are there to help them and are their best immediate chance of resolving the situation. This simple statement often helps defuse the situation.
- **Don't take it personally:** Always speak to the issue at hand and do not get personal, even if the customer does. Remember that the customer doesn't know you and is just venting frustration at you as a representative of your company. Gently guide the conversation back to the issue and how you intend to resolve it.
- **Remember that you're interacting with a human:** Everyone has an occasional bad day. Maybe your rude customer had a fight with their spouse, got a traffic ticket that morning or had a recent run of bad luck. We've all been there, to some degree. Try to empathize and make their day better by being a pleasant, calming voice – it'll make you feel good, too.

- **If you promise a callback, call back:** Even if you promised an update that you don't have yet, call the customer at the scheduled time anyway. The customer will be reassured that you are not trying to dodge them and will appreciate the follow-up.
- **Summarize the next steps:**At the end of the call, let the customer know exactly what to expect, and then be sure to follow through on your promises. Document the call to ensure you're well prepared for the next interaction.

CHAPTER NINE

Restaurant Floor Plan Guideline

Your restaurant floor plan is essentially a map of your restaurant's physical space. When designed well, your restaurant floor plan can affect your profit margins by increasing efficiency, creating ease of movement, securing the safety of your staff and guests, and ultimately enhancing your customer experience.

The fundamental component of any restaurant interior is the chair and the table. Depending upon restaurant type, menu, service table setting, and the degree of intimacy required, table size and overall chair space requirements can and should vary considerably. A restaurant that encourages the rapid turnover of customers will typically provide a smaller tabletop and chair. On the other hand, restaurants that encourage limited turnover and emphasize the wining and dining experience will usually offer larger tabletop sizes and more comfortable chairs.

Apart from the anthropometrical and ergonomic requirements, there are many other design factors that play an influential role in designing an optimum floor plan for a restaurant. These are namely –

- Circulation and egress- This is the movement of the people, how the staff and the customers can move around and enter and exit the restaurant.
- Methods of service (self or monitored)- The restaurant design will very much depend on whether the staff would serve the food, or if it is a self-service restaurant.
- The overall dimension of the given space- The restaurant design heavily depends upon the whole proportion and area available. Based on this, the architect would draft the restaurant design and create a floor plan.

You need to hire an architect or an interior designer who would help you with your restaurant design and floor plan. The architect would be able to come up with the spatial configurations and draw up the floor plans to make sure that the restaurant layout is safe with the most pleasant ambiance. He will be the one dealing with where and how to build a wall, design a staircase, and how to structure and collaborate various elements and principles of design in generating a harmonious and functional floor plan.

A restaurant floor plan is a blueprint that illustrates the distance and relationships between the rooms and physical structures of your restaurant space. Restaurant floor plans denote the locations of fixtures like furnaces, sinks, water heaters, and electrical outlets. Occasionally, they will also include annotations on which materials are used to build parts of the space and how parts of the space are built.

Your architect or interior designer will draw up your floor plan. A well-designed floor plan will include:

- Walls and hallways
- Closets and storage spaces
- Restrooms
- Windows and doors
- Set fixtures and appliances such as stoves, refrigerators, water heaters, etc.
- The purpose of each room / space
- Interior features such as fixed shelving, counter space, bars, etc.
- Other important items in your restaurant's space

A well-designed floor plan will serve to:

- Increase efficiency and workflow
- Help you stick to your budget as you build your restaurant
- Help you train your staff to work as cohesively and efficiently as possible

Your restaurant layout is also important for operational flow. This refers to all the foot traffic in your restaurant, including where deliveries are picked up, how chefs move around the kitchen area, where servers pick up orders, and more.

Here are some guidelines for figuring out the average square footage you need per customer, depending on your venue type:

- Fine dining: 18–20 square feet

- Full service restaurant: 12–15 square feet
- Fast casual: 11–14 square feet
- Fast food: 11–14 square feet

In a 1,200 square foot dining space, you could fit up to 80–100 seats, depending on the experience you're trying to create for your customers.

ALLOCATING PRIMARY SPACE: When considering primary spaces for your restaurant floor plan, the general rule of thumb for determining the allotted area is that the dining room should comprise most of the total space. The remaining space should be allocated to kitchen, storage and preparation area. These dimensions may have to be updated and adjusted if your floor plans include a waiting or bar area. However, those spaces should be the approximate percentages for the area.

Space Total Area

Dining Room 60% total area

Kitchen, preparation, storage 40% total area

ESTAURANT FURNITURE SPACING GUIDELINES

For safety assurance and to allow for the free flow of traffic for customers and servers there needs to be a minimum space allowance for the traffic path between the various furniture items. Below are some guidelines served to assist you in determining the ideal seating space and table height you should consider:

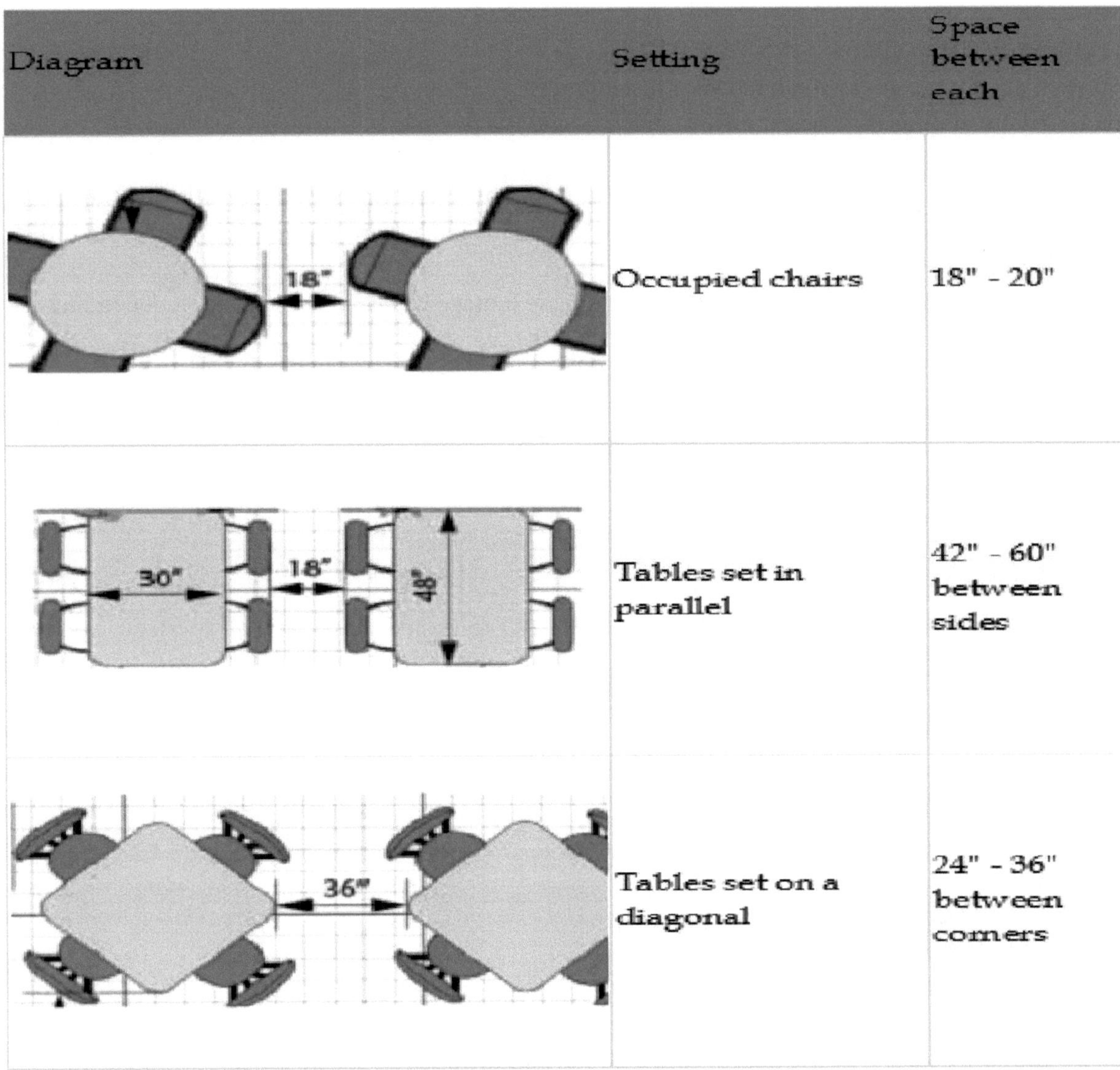

Diagram	Setting	Space between each
18"	Occupied chairs	18" - 20"
30" 18" 48"	Tables set in parallel	42" - 60" between sides
36"	Tables set on a diagonal	24" - 36" between corners

Enter Caption

One thing to remember when planning your layout and purchasing the furniture is to match the tables and seating heights

Table Height Seating Height

Table Height: 29″ – 30″ Chair Seat Height: 17″ – 18″

Bar Height: 36″ – 42″ Bar Stool Seat Height: 29″ – 30″

Features a Restaurant Design and Floor Plan

The space requirements for the restaurant design must always be kept in mind. Below are a few of the essential features that one should keep in mind to make any restaurant design and floor plan efficient.

Human Comfort: Human comfort in an indoor space primarily relies on thermal comfort and indoor air quality (achieved by temperature, humidity control good and ventilation), lighting, and acoustic comfort. Apart from these, the floor plan must be such that space available for design should be able to provide each customer with comfortable personal space. There must be enough space in the design to sit, stand, walk in, and walk out comfortably.

Thermal Comfort and Indoor Air Quality: The internal heat gains are very high in all restaurants (especially in kitchens) due to cooking, lighting, electrical equipment, and the number of clients. HVAC (heating ventilation and air conditioning) forms an important feature and consideration for achieving a functional restaurant design.

Lighting: Lighting Design aims to enable the occupant to work and move around in safety. It provides for our visual needs, and also safety and security. People intuitively know that light affects their mood. The challenge while designing lighting is to understand under what circumstances certain visual conditions might be better than others and to use that knowledge to create lighting systems that improve overall performance and human comfort. Light in restaurants can be divided into three categories- Ambient, Accent, and Mood Lighting. While ambient lighting is used for normal functions, accent lighting is focused on a particular area. Mood lighting is for the aesthetic, and it is the combination of these three that define light in restaurant design. In restaurant interior design psychology, lighting is considered an essential factor, and the restaurant design focuses on the function and psychological impact of various lights. The floor plan must be designed in cahoots with the overall effect and placing of each of these light elements.

Acoustic: People are talking, background noise or sound, and the architectural design of the restaurant itself affects the overall acoustical quality of the space. The variety of ambient music in a restaurant straightaway regulates the user experience and, ultimately, the feedback. The average noise level of a typical restaurant during a dining rush is 80 db.

Restaurants traditionally have carpeted floors and soft furnishings and upholstered chairs, tablecloths, and curtains which provide sound-absorbing qualities. Recent trends lean towards a modern look, which generally includes high ceilings and hard surfaces; though these features are aesthetically pleasing, they are known to produce excessive room echo. As these venues are usually fast-paced and crowded, this makes for an uncomfortably loud environment. A study shows that more booming bars increase the amount and pace of alcohol consumed. Still, for a restaurant, a balance needs to be created concerning aesthetics and desired acoustical levels for ultimate human comfort.

Optimum Utilization of Seating and Smooth Circulation: The space design plan should be made in such a way that it allows the servers to move quickly with food and beverages in the restaurant and also allows the guests to move in and out of the restaurant freely. Floor plans should also provide customers with enough elbow room. The areas for specific functions need to be decided in such a way that the seating space is maximized without compromising the customers' level of comfort. Allocating enough space to work comfortably and efficiently in each area is essential. Your restaurant floor layout should focus on the comfort and enjoyment of your customers while maintaining an efficient circulation pattern.

Safety Concerns: Restaurant design standards require that there should be sufficient space between tables. For instance, if there's an emergency, and you need to evacuate the building, having clear pathways to the exits is an integral part of keeping everyone safe. Full paths should be built to avoid employees and guests alike tripping and hurting themselves as they navigate your dining room.

Basic Requirements: Although specific layouts vary according to the type and size of the restaurant, most floor plans include similar components. The spatial arrangement within the floor plan should be in such a way that there are two primary functional spaces. These are "the front of the house"- constituting the entrance, waiting for the lobby, POS, Dining area, Bar/Lounge are well connected to "the back of the house"- representing the kitchen, pantry, storage, service entry, and administration areas. The designer needs to find a balance between connectivity and privacy in this area. It is essential to understand that the back of the house and its functioning needs to be hidden from the customers. This is one of the most critical parts of a restaurant design plan.

The Entrance: The entrance of your restaurant casts the first impression of your restaurant on the customer. The entry gives a preview of the type of space a patron is going to enter. A well-designed restaurant design plan should ideally provide ample space that is welcoming and should evoke curiosity in the customer to come in and dine. The act of entering can be signified in more subtle ways than just puncturing a hole in the wall. The entry can be an elaborate one that emphasizes the opening or can bring forth the theme of the restaurant.

Your Restaurant Entrance should be:

Able to draw people in and make them feel immediately comfortable.

Well maintained & easy to open.

It is inviting and welcoming.

While evaluating your entrance, focus on these components:

Does the design allow staff to greet people well?

Does the entrance make customers feel welcome?

Does it allow a free-flowing circulation for customers as well as the staff?

Dining Room Layouts: The dining area of a restaurant is the soul of the place. The customer spends 98% of the time in this area. While designing the dining room layout, your primary aim should be that your customers be comfortable in the seating area and enjoy their food. Your interiors in the dining area have to be designed depending on the concept and the theme of your restaurant. This, of course, would also depend on the space available and the theme of the restaurant. Your dining area setting should be in sync with the theme of your restaurant.

Seating Area: The seating area should be designed with at least three sizes of tables with the motive to accommodate small, medium, and large parties accordingly. The window area space can be used for small two-person tables. Similarly, the middle section can be best utilized for accommodating larger parties. Between every dining table, there should be a standard of 3-4 ft to avoid any chaos and disturbance. There should be ample space that allows for the free and seamless movement of the servers.

Waiting Area: The waiting area is often overlooked while creating restaurant designs. Disregarding this area results in diners waiting for the table. There should be enough space for guests where they could wait for dining.

POS terminals or Billing System Area: The POS system should be positioned at a place that will maximize efficiency. There should be a minimization of the staff running back and forth between the payment stations. Your restaurant design should be structured to get as many

tables as you can into your dining room. The number of tables could greatly affect how many tables turn (and checks) you have in a shift.

The Kitchen: One of the most important components of your Restaurant Design and Floor Plan is your Kitchen Area. The kitchen is designed primarily by taking into consideration the views of the Head chef, kitchen consultant, architect, and contracting firm representative. The kitchen consultant is responsible for the design and usually providing the kitchen items like Stainless steel units, suitable chimneys, freezing units, and others. The electrical and plumbing services are provided by the contracting firm with a consultation of the kitchen consultant and the architect. A well-laid-out kitchen will make your staff happy and more efficient in their work.

The kitchen design of the restaurant design and floor plan should ideally have the following aspects:

- Specific kitchen working zones- Specific kitchen working zones should be defined in the kitchen floor plan. Namely, pre-preparation area, food assembly and packing, and washing area.
- Designated spaces- The kitchen and food storage areas include designated spaces for cooking equipment, food preparation, and dishwashing, as well as cold and dry food storage.
- The moving area in the kitchen- The layout shall be made in such a way that allows the kitchen staff to move in quickly, swiftly, and efficiently. Providing enough space is critical to avoid accidents as well.
- Proper ventilation– Ensure adequate ventilation in your restaurant kitchen as it is necessary for the health of your restaurant staff and also reduces the chances of the various items being prepared in the kitchen waft to the dining area.
- Employees restrooms: You may also choose to include an office, employee bathrooms, or a break room in the back of the house.

Allocating Adequate Space for Different Areas In The Kitchen

An efficient Restaurant kitchen floor plan shall include adequate space for receiving and storing goods, inventory, water closet, prep areas, cooking stations, food storage, water closet, dishwashing zone, inventory, equipment. It is suggested that equipment with similar functions should be stored together, and after their use, they should be kept in their proper place.

Kitchen Cooking Area: This is one of the most critical zones of the kitchen area, where the actual food preparation will take place. All the equipment like burners, oven, grills, tandoor and other equipment needed for the operations pre-decided will have to be positioned in this area.

Prep Area: This is the area where most of your kitchen prep happens. The prep area needs to be well equipped to accommodate all the ingredients required for the preparation of the food.

Storage Area: The storage area should be well equipped to store all the dry goods that are mostly bought in bulk, such as rice, flour, sugar, lentils, oils, whole spices, and spice powders. This space shall be designed and maintained so that it is moisture-free and free of pests and rodents. The store area is generally designed adjacent to the kitchen. It serves as a facility storage facility for both the kitchen and dining items of the restaurant.

Cold Storage : Another crucial element of the kitchen design is the cold storage area. There is a continuous need for cold rooms, deep freezers, and perishables to stock perishables like meat, seafood, and frozen food. The facilities that you would need in your cold storage will depend on the quantity the restaurant handles. The maintenance of cold storage also needs to be done.

Washing Area: The washing area in the restaurant should be allotted the maximum space for the workflow to be smooth. The washing space should be equipped to accommodate washing of large cooking vessels, cutlery, crockery, and other utensils. There should also be a space where the used cutlery, crockery, utensils would be kept for washing.

Pantry Area: A pantry is a room or a ready to serve area where beverages, food, and sometimes dishes and others as decided by the head chef.

Staff Personal Area: There should be a space for a staff toilet. A small area can also be created for staff where they could change their uniforms and keep their personal belongings or things they would need for their use.

Restrooms: It is undisputed that the restaurant owners need to pay ample attention to the food and services offered by them, but at the same time, the cleanliness of the restaurant, especially the restrooms, forms an integral part of the customer's dining experience. The toilets should ideally be divided into male and female sections. Give special attention to this area as it is usually ignored in the restaurant planning and design stage. Restrooms leave a lasting impression on the mind of the customer.

They should have sufficient lighting and easy to clean and maintain. Every customer will appreciate sparkling, clean, and large enough restrooms to accommodate multiple guests.

Keep the Following Points in Mind

The restrooms should be easy to access for the customers without unnecessary wandering.

It is advisable that the restrooms shall also have wheelchair access for catering to the specific needs of physically challenged customers.

It is necessary that the restaurant restrooms should be appropriately equipped with sanitation facilities, especially trash disposal, and have proper designated space on the bathroom floor plan.

The restrooms should also be equipped with proper lighting.

Electrical Services: The electrical part of the restaurant is a fundamental and crucial aspect of both the operations and safety of the establishment. Depending on the location, the wiring, termination, lighting fixtures, cabling need to be taken care of both professionally and diligently. Plan the site for the central control panels, Generators, etc. systematically.

Restaurant floor plans are ultimately a balancing act between various functional needs and requirements of restaurant design. Designing your restaurant floor plan might seem a little easier task as compared to financing, licensing, or construction that goes along with starting a business. But the restaurant floor plan is a critical aspect of effective restaurant design.

You know your restaurant floor plan is reduced when there have been instances in your restaurant when any customer might have smacked his head with a server while passing through a tight corner, or a customer might have had to sit with a stranger to let someone else pass through the aisle way. Therefore, you should always avoid these disastrous situations by analyzing your restaurant design requirements and specific needs before finalizing the layout.

CHAPTER TEN

SEQUENCE OF SERVICE IN RESTAURANT

Courtesy is one of the most essential aspects of restaurant service, especially in upmarket operations. Efforts must be made to ensure a relaxed and welcoming atmosphere with a warm, friendly and efficient service provided with politeness. The sequence of service is referred to as the order in which a waiter provides service to guests from the time the guest enters the restaurant to the time he leaves the restaurant. Preparation to deliver satisfying service begins before the guest steps into the restaurant with activities like handling reservation, allocation of the table, F&B service, farewell etc... Once the guest arrives in the restaurant there is a certain sequence that is followed to make his/ her meal experience pleasant.

Handling Reservation & Allocation of tables:

Reservations are accepted in fine dining or speciality restaurants; coffee shop does not accept reservations. Following points must be noted down while taking down a reservation:

Name of the guest

No. of pax

Time of reservation

Contact number and name of the booker

Any special request/ requirement

Table preference.

Reservations of the day are discussed during the briefing prior to meal period; allocation of the tables is done at this time. Allocation of the table is done prior to the arrival of the guest and a note of the same is made on the reservation register, so that;

The guests can be seated on the appropriate table, as per request or occasion.

All restaurant staff is aware of the same, thereby eliminating confusion and ensuring smooth and professional welcome.

Ensuring optimum seating levels in the restaurant.

Welcoming The Guest: However the restaurant staff may seek spontaneity and friendliness, certain rituals are a must while welcoming a guest to the restaurant.

As the guest enters a restaurant, he/ she must be greeted cordially and must be made to feel comfortable. Usually this task is performed by the hostess of the restaurant, however, is not just restricted to her. It is for each and every restaurant staff to see to it that the guest is greeted within 30 seconds of arriving in the restaurant.

Guest must be greeted with a clear and affable tone of voice, good appearance and a smile. Every guest must be welcomed with the greeting of the day, i.e. Good Morning/ Good afternoon/ Good Evening.

If the guest is regular then must be greeted with name, i.e. 'Good morning Mr. Gajanan'. Greeting phrases differ from restaurant to restaurant. In ethnic restaurants, the guest is greeted in the national/ regional greeting.

In case the restaurant staff is busy serving other guests, they must ensure that even though they may not be physically free to welcome guest, they must acknowledge their presence by a smile or a gesture to say "We will be with you in a minute". Never ignore the guests.

Find out if the guest has a reservation:

If yes -> Then escort them to their table and address them by their name, should they not be satisfied with the table then offer alternatives.

If No -> then ask them for their preference of table and escort them to the table. Guest should be led to their table, if there is a gesture towards the table, it must be done with an open palm facing upwards rather than pointing a finger on to the table.

Seating the guest:

- It is guests' prerogative to choose where they want to sit or where their host would like them to sit.
- Ladies must be seated first.

- Seating the guest on a chair Stands straight 9-12" behind the guests' chair.
- Bring the right foot forward, with the knee touching the wooden skirting of the seat in the middle. Hold the chair from both the hands from the sides of the back.
- Lift the chair about 1" from behind and pull it back, ensuring that there is adequate space for the guests to go between the table and chair.
- When the guest proceeds to sit down, move the chair slowly towards the guest, till it is comfortable for the guest and rest the chair of the floor.
- It must be ensured that the chair is not dragged.
- Seating the guest on a sofa If space is not sufficient for the guests to move in, move the table outside and place it back in position as soon as the guests have sat down.
- If the table is heavy then the waiter must ask for assistance from his colleagues, under no circumstances the guests' help should be sought.

Pouring water

As soon as the guests are seated, the waiter must pour water. Guests' must be asked for their preference of water (regular, mineral, aerated, spring water) and while pouring water following points must be kept in mind:

- Regular water poured from a water jug Jug should be clean with sufficient water for the number of people on the table.
- Should be cold and room temperature as per the guest's requirement.
- Should be carried on an underliner or with a waiters' cloth neatly folded to ensure that the condensed water does not drip on the table.
- Water must be served from the right-hand side, ladies must be served first.

- Glasses must only be refilled when they are two-thirds empty.
- Mineral water poured from the bottle Seal must be opened in front of the guest.
- Should be carried in a cane basket and after pouring can be placed back on the table.
- However, must be ensured that the service of water is done by the staff and not be the guests themselves.
- Guests must be checked with, before opening a new bottle.

Order taking

Aperitif card must be presented to take drink order prior to presenting food menu. Unless the food has been pre-ordered, as soon as the guests are seated, they must be presented with the menu card.

- Presenting a menu card Present individual menu cards to the guests.
- Menu card must be presented from the right-hand side, open to the first page.
- Give 5-7 minutes to the guests to go through the menu.
- Check with the guests if they are ready to place the order, by inquiring " May I take your order Sir/ Madam" or " Are you ready to place your order Sir/ Madam"? Stand straight at a position where it is convenient to talk to the guests.

- Assist the guest in choosing the best dish on offer, use 'suggestive selling' or 'upselling' techniques.
- Takedown the order systematically on KOT (Kitchen Order Ticket) After taking order, repeat the order.
- Take menu card back from the guests and put it back in place.
- Inform the guests of the approximate time it would take to serve the food.

Service of Food and Beverage orders
Service of Beverage:

- Beverages are served first.
- Always serve beverages from the right of the guest.
- While the guests are waiting for their meal, bread and butter must be served immediately.
- Waiting staff must ensure that the same is replenished as soon as it is over.
- The guest should not have to ask for it.
- Before serving the food the waiters must ensure that the cover is appropriate, should it need to be changed then it must be done before the food comes to the table.
- This must be done discreetly, ensuring minimum intrusion and disturbance to guest and with minimum cluttering. Food order must be announced before the service.

The sequence of serving guest is as following:

1. Guest of honour is served first.
2. A lady in the party takes precedence over the male guest of honour.
3. Ladies must be served before Gentlemen.
4. Older people are served before younger ones.
5. The host must be served last.

Service of food:

- Pre-plated service of food must be from the right-hand side.
- Once the food is placed the covers must be adjusted if the tableware is disturbed.
- Platter to plate or silver service must be from the left-hand side.
- Service of each course should be co-ordinated in a manner that the guests do not have to wait for a long time between the courses.

- Guest must be asked whether the food is up to their expectation.
- It must not happen that in enthusiasm, 3-4 people go to the guest to ask if 'everything is alright'! This may irritate the guest and may be an intrusion on his privacy.
- Water and other food items must be served/ replenished as soon as it is over.
- Before removing anything from the tale, seek guest's permission.

Clearance

- Used plates are cleared from the right-hand side.
- Plates are cleared after all the guests on the table have finished their meal.
- Indication for closing the meal is done by placing a knife and fork together across the plate.

- Clearance is done by the right hand and collected on the left hand, by the 'first plate' technique.
- Ensure that all the dishes are cleared from the table.

- Ensure that that cruet set, butter dish, bread boat, cutlery unused by the guest is removed from the table.
- Do not remove bud vase ashtray and glasses from the table.
- All dirties should be taken for dishwashing except cruet set, which must be left on the side station.

Crumbing

- Crumbing is done to remove spills or crumbs on the table after a course or after the main course, prior to dessert being served.
- Carried out by a crumbing spade, crumbing brush or on a B&B plate with a waiters' cloth and a B&B knife to pick up gravies that might have fallen on the tablecloth.
- Begin crumbing from the left-hand side, holding the plate on the left hand just under the tabletop; gently sweep the crumbs on to the plate.

- Open the dessertspoon and dessert fork.
- Bad stains can be covered with a clean white napkin.

Dessert order/ Tea Coffee Order

Similar procedure as order taking a waiter can take the opportunity to suggest Liqueurs or and other digestive as this time.

Presenting the check

- Checks must be presented only when asked.
- The waiter must bring the check-in a neat and tidy folder.
- Guest comment card should be in the folder.
- A pen must be given along with the check folder.
- When the guest is leaving the folder must be removed very discreetly.
- Tips must never be solicited (ask for or try to obtain).

Guest Feedback

Taking the Feedback from the guest about the food and service.

Farewell

- This is as crucial as welcoming the guest.
- Guest must be helped in getting up by pulling out the chair for them.
- Should be assisted with coats/ shawls.
- Must be thanked, Must be welcomed again. Eg: "Look forward to welcoming you back to the restaurant", "We hope that you visit us soon".

A-la-carte service sequence

Service of soup

- Soup is plated and served from the right-hand side
- Place soup accompaniment before serving the soup. the place just above the fork.
- Take soup bowls and under plates on a salver to the table.

- Stand to the right of the guest, keeping tray behind the guest.
- Place bowl on the under plate, take the soup and place it from the right-hand side and announce the name of the soup.

- If a soup cup is in use, the handles of the cup should be towards the left and the right-hand side of the guest
- Move clockwise to the next guest and repeat
- Serve the host last.

Service of fish

- Serve fish on the half plate and can be either plated or silver served.
- Keep the necessary accompaniments for fish.
- Serve white wine if ordered.

If pre-plated

- Collect the fish on a half plate from the kitchen and place it from the right-hand side.

If platter to plate

- Carry a pile of half plates on the flat of left palm over a serviette to the table.
- place plate from the right-hand side
- Move clockwise to the next guest and repeat till you place a plate for the host.
- Collect the fish dishes from the kitchen and take them to the table.
- Take the dish closer to the guest's plate from the left-hand side.
- Using a service spoon and fork serve fish on the plate and move counterclockwise to the next guest.
- Serve the host last

Service of the main course

- A large plate is used for the main course and pieces of cutlery used are a large knife and fork.
- Make sure the cover has required cutlery

Pre-plated

- Collect the main dish on a full plate from the kitchen and place it on the right-hand side (The plate will have meat, potatoes, vegetables arranged in the kitchen).
- Place plate in such a way that the meat is closer to the guest, at 6 o'clock position on the plate.
- Move clockwise to the next guest.
- Serve host last
- Serve roast gravy from the sauceboat with sauce ladle from the left-hand side and after serving everyone, place the sauceboat on an underplate on the table

Platter to plate

- Carry a pile of full plates on the flat of the left palm over a serviette to the table.
- Place plate from the right-hand side (use waiter's cloth)
- Move clockwise to the next guest and repeat till you place the plate for the host.
- Collect the main dish and accompanying vegetables and potatoes from the kitchen and place them on the sideboard
- Take the meat dish to the table and using a service spoon and fork, serve meat on the plate from the left-hand side and move counter-clockwise to the next guest.

- Place The meat closer to the guest at the 6 o'clock position on the plate.
- Take back the meat to the sideboard and place it on the hot plate,
- Take potatoes and accompanying vegetable dishes from the sideboard, each with its own service spoon and fork, on a salver to the guests.
- Serve potatoes first on the full plate at 12 o'clock position with service spoon and fork from the left-hand side.
- Roted the salver so that the vegetable dish is closer to the guest's plate.
- Move counter-clockwise to the next guest and serve as mentioned above and repeat
- Serve the host last

Rules in service

1. Always serve kids first followed by ladies and gentlemen.
2. serve the host at last.
3. While serving avoid close proximity to the guest.
4. You should not cross the guest while serving or clearing.
5. While serving on the left the left leg should be placed forward and on right and the right leg should be forward.
6. When serving an order "Excuse yourself". This will inform the guest that you are ready to serve his order and he will give way.
7. All beverages and the pre-plated dish should be served from the right side of the guest.
8. Platter to plate service always done from the left and clear from right.
9. Always use round salver for beverage service.
10. Water should be chilled unless asked otherwise.
11. If only beverage is served, it is placed in front of the guest otherwise to the right side of the cover.
12. Hot beverages like tea, coffee. and milk are served in a cup and saucer in a dolly paper with tea spoon.
13. Prior to soup service make sure that bread rolls in the breadbasket and butter in butter pot is placed on the table for soup.
14. Whenever applicable serve cold items before hot items.

1. Serve cold dishes on a cold plate and hot dishes on hot plate.
2. While serving a dish the manipulation of the silver should be such that the service spoon is below and the serving fork on top.
3. Serving platter or entree dish should have folded waiter's cloth underneath. It should not be in direct contact with the palm.
4. While serving, serving cutleries should not touch the guest's plate.
5. Bring the platter as close as possible to the guest's plate to avoid drippings while serving.
6. Indian bread and all varieties of pappads should be served in the side plate/B&B/quarter plate.
7. Rice should be served slightly away from the centre towards the bottom of the plate.
8. You should not pile the food on the guest's plate while serving.
9. Before serving of dessert or whenever the table becomes dirty crumbling down should be done with a crumb scooper or waiter's clothe.

CHAPTER ELEVEN

Developing Unique Selling Proposition

When someone mentions a restaurant by name, you probably respond with something like That's the place that serves best kebabs or "That's the one with the relaxed atmosphere." Those are both USPs. They are part of each restaurant's concept and the traits that stick in customers' minds.

The following strategies will help you discover and pitch your unique characteristics to capture your ideal customer.

Find Your Niche: Start by crafting your restaurant's unique selling proposition. If you can't immediately pinpoint or differentiate what you do best and how that differs from others, sit down and think it through.

Here are some characteristics that may apply to you:

Qualities Your gourmet cuisine has been recognized with awards and reviews.

Sustainability You only use locally-sourced ingredients and grow your own herbs.

Value You offer the best prices in your area.

Service From wait staff to online ordering, you've perfected the art of great customer service.

Signature Dish There are one or two dishes you have created that are completely original.

Traditional Fare Your food is made from family recipes, or you use ethnically-specific techniques or spices.

Ambiance Your dining room's décor and atmosphere is distinctive (i.e., intimate, hip, family-friendly)

Convenience You've streamlined operations to offer easy online ordering and fast delivery times.

Who Is Your Customer?

The next step is to determine who your unique offerings will resonate with. Don't try to be all things to all people. This dilutes your strengths and prevents you from targeting your ideal customers.

For instance, a family-friendly atmosphere and menu, and discounted prices may not appeal to affluent empty-nesters looking for a refined dining experience. Nor will these characteristics attract millennials craving health-conscious, ethnically diverse cuisine.

Conversely, busy families will be attracted to dining rooms where they'll feel comfortable bringing their fussy youngsters. They will also need to satisfy their need for kid-friendly menu items and value.

Whatever your assets may be, diners are out there tailor made for you.

Messages That Stand Out

People make decisions about where to eat every day, with increasingly more options to choose from. Here are some ideas to help you craft your unique selling proposition to tell your story effectively and make your restaurant irresistible:

Sum it up. Create a one or two-sentence phrase that communicates your uniqueness. Make your ***value proposition*** clear to the customer (unlike a slogan, which is typically just catchy, without necessarily expressing value). In other words, state what's in it for the customer. Use this phrase in your marketing messages.

Create Concise Messages. When communicating your unique selling point, get to the point quickly! For instance, 40-character Facebook, and 100-character Twitter posts have shown to have higher engagement rates.

Be creative. Find a way to express your unique selling point in a memorable way, using your own distinct brand personality. Perhaps a series of YouTube videos will help you set the tone for your brand.

Follow Through

Here are several things you can do to make sure every aspect of your restaurant lives up to your promise:

Menu. Make any necessary tweaks so your menu reflects your brand personality in content and style. For instance, delete items that don't align with your brand. Also, use colors, fonts, images and descriptive copy that appeals to your target customer.

Innovation. Adjust operations to deliver on the expectations you've set. For instance, if your value proposition is to make customers' lives easier, have systems in place to back that up: online ordering and tracking, alternative payments, etc.

Training. Make sure your unique selling proposition resonates internally with your staff. Set clear objectives and guidelines to help them represent your brand successfully.

These techniques will help you fully utilize your inherent strengths to attract and retain a customer base that values and rewards your uniqueness.

CHAPTER TWELVE

Menu Engineering

Although you likely have a target overall food cost in your establishment, not every menu item will carry exactly the same food cost percentage. Some items are more costly than others, but most establishments will have a range of prices that all the menu items fit into. Consequently, it is important to balance the menu so that the low and high food cost items work together to help you reach your target food cost. This process is called menu engineering. **Menu engineering** means balancing the high and low food cost items; it also includes strategically featuring or promoting items to help reach your targets.

In the menu engineering field, common terminology groups together different levels of profitability and popularity to form the following groups:

- **Plowhorses: Low Profitability and High Popularity.** These are menu items that do not have a high profit margin but are crowd-pleasers, making them essential to keep on your menu. A classic example is steak or fresh-caught, unique fish. You might consider using less expensive ingredients or decreasing the portion size to make it more profitable. If the item continues to have a small profit margin, you should avoid upselling or featuring it on your menu.
- **Dogs: Low Profitability and Low Popularity.** Dogs represent food items that are not ordered often nor have a large profit margin. Consider removing these items from your menu. However, there are cases when you may want to keep Dogs on your menu. One example may be kids' options, such as a grilled cheese or kiddie burger, which may not sell often but are important to keep on your menu for families. If continuing to offer items in this category, avoid upselling or accentuating them on your menu.
- **Stars: High Profitability and High Popularity.** These are the items that have a high profit margin and that are frequently ordered by guests. Typical examples include pasta or popular

cocktails, like margaritas. You should showcase these the most on your menu, promote them, and avoid drastically changing the ingredients of these dishes.

- **Puzzles: High Profitability and Low Popularity.** Puzzles are items that have a high profit margin but are hard to sell. The recipes of these items may need to be tweaked to appeal to guests. Additionally, servers should upsell these menu items, and menu engineers would recommend finding ways to highlight them on your menu.

Restructure and Redesign Your Menu

To turn over a greater profit, psychologists and menu engineers have identified a series of menu engineering strategies that encourage guests to spend more and to select high profit items. These strategies include emphasizing certain items and muting the costs of dishes. Below are the most valuable menu engineering tips.

1. **Guide guests' attention to your high profit items.** Studies show that customers are likely to order one of the first items that draws their attention. Since guests only spend an average of 109 seconds looking at your menu, it must be designed for guests to easily find key items.

- **Use an attention-grabbing technique.** Include a photo, graphic, colored or shaded box, border, or surround the item(s) with white space. Only highlight one or two items per section.
- **Place the items you want to sell in the center, the top right corner, and the top left corner.** Psychologists fittingly call these three areas "The Golden Triangle," and it refers to the way our eyes tend to move when first looking at a menu.
- **In each section, place your most profitable items at the top of the list and one at the bottom.** Studies show that people notice and order the top two items or the last item in each section more often than the others.

2. **Include a "decoy" menu item that would seem overly expensive to guests.** Place this near your high profit margin items.

They may already have a reasonable price, but when compared to the "decoy" item, they will appear even more attractive. Or, put a "decoy" item next to your high-profit, pricey items that would seem more reasonable when compared to the "decoy" item(s).

1. **On a similar note, try "bracketing".** Include two portion options for one dish without including the exact size. The "larger" size will have a steeper price, such as INR-110, while the "smaller" size will have a seemingly cheaper price, like INR-128. The customer won't know exactly how much smaller the small portion is, yet it will still seem to be the best-value price, since it simply costs less. In reality, the "smaller" portion can be the one you wanted to sell the whole time, and this tactic makes the meal item more attractive because guests will feel they are choosing a dish with good value.
2. **Write your pricing information using the nesting method.** List the price discreetly after each meal description in the same size font, so customers' eyes glide right over the price instead of focusing on it. Avoid the below tactics:

   - **Avoid ending your prices with .99.** This can sound cheap and unsatisfying to many customers.
   - **Avoid dollar signs.** Currency indicators remind customers that they're spending money and can even make them feel like they are spending more than they are. Soften the price by eliminating the dollar sign.
   - **Avoid price trails.** Price trails are dotted lines that connect your menu items to their price, which is often listed on the other side of the page. This takes the focus away from your dish description and straight to the price instead.
   - **Avoid price columns.** By placing your prices in a column next to your dishes, guests can easily compare prices and may make their decision based on the cheapest dish.

3. Use selective, descriptive language. Many diners will make their final decisions off of this information. Descriptive menu labels lead to customers feeling more satisfied with their meals, and appetizing descriptions can also offset a high price.

Menu Designing Tips

Guests will only scan your menu for an average of 109 seconds. This means you have a small amount of time to set your menu's tone for both customer satisfaction and optimal profit. Below are the basics to ease your customers' experience based on psychology research of menu design.

- **Use color.** People respond to color in emotional, subconscious ways, so choose your color scheme accordingly.

  - Bright colors like red, yellow, and orange capture attention and trigger appetite. You can use this to attract attention to specific areas of your menu and create a hierarchy for the layout.

  - You can also match your color scheme to your restaurant's theme to reinforce associations. For example, use light blue to highlight the ocean-caught fish at your seafood restaurant, or use green and tan for a farm-to-table restaurant.

- **Make your menu scannable.** Avoid crowded layouts, and choose an easy-to-read font and font size. Include clear section headings and visible dish titles. Even if your menu is more than one or two pages, menu engineers would agree that if your menu is scannable with fewer choices per category, guests will still feel at ease when making a choice from your menu.
- **Limit choices.** The "paradox of choice" states that the more options we have, the more anxiety we feel. Psychologists suggest that restaurateurs limit options per category to around 7 items.
- **Invoke nostalgia or humanize dishes in another way.** These menu items are attractive because customers feel like they're ordering something special, and they induce happy memories of childhood or feelings of comfort and closeness. Examples: "Grandma's Chocolate Chip Cookie," "Campfire Hot Chocolate," or references to the chef or restaurant owner, such as "Chef Mike's Charbroiled Steak."
- **Include a separate dessert menu.** If guests see an eye-catching dessert, they are more likely to skip an appetizer. By surprising guests with your dessert menu after dinner, you are more likely to obtain appetizer and dessert sales.

- **Use photos sparingly or not at all.** Excessive photos are associated with low-end, cheap venues, so high-end restaurants usually avoid photos. However, one photo per page has been shown to increase sales up to 30%, especially at casual, affordable eateries. If you still want to share more photos of your dishes, your Instagram or Facebook pages can do this for you.
- **Choose a reasonable menu size.** Physically oversized menus can be uncomfortable for guests to maneuver. Ensure your menu is easy to handle and can be easily placed on tables.

Revamping your menu with menu engineering tactics can greatly improve your restaurant profits, and menu psychology techniques can improve the experience of your guests.

Use mouthwatering words to amp up your menu descriptions

Which sounds better: a burger and fries or a char-grilled Angus beef burger with aged cheddar and hand-cut Idaho fries?

Your menu descriptions should be concise but descriptive. If that sounds contradictory, just think of maximizing your space. Make every word matter. Longer isn't necessarily better, but if an adjective or specific name of a product will help sell a menu item, then there's likely value in including it in your description.

For starters, emphasize "yummy words" that are likely to get customers' stomachs rumbling. Salads are crispy and fresh, barbecue is sticky-sweet and smoky, and desserts are perfectly flaky with a sinful chocolate drizzle. Consider your demographic, too; if you're catering to an audience that appreciates locally sourced produce or sustainability, work in related buzzwords.

CHAPTER THIRTEEN

Production Basics

Your restaurant kitchen is that inevitable part of your restaurant which single-handedly decides the success of your establishment. Think of it as a battery of a car. If it is kept in good condition with regular analyses and maintenance, the car runs smoothly. Ever since the restaurant world adapted to modern technologies, kitchen management is no longer a headache.

The back-of-house operations of a restaurant are always the **busiest** and the **most hectic.** Basically, the restaurant kitchen. It is not your everyday kitchen. In a restaurant kitchen, food is prepared on a large scale. Multiple batches of the same dish are made throughout the entirety of a day. The kitchen staff is always on their toes creating and recreating enjoyable meals for customers. The pressure is naturally more when chefs get repeat orders.

Keeping in mind the significance of a kitchen in a restaurant, **kitchen management becomes an inescapable task.** Therefore, how one must manage a restaurant kitchen effectively? What are the challenges faced by restaurateurs? And since it's not a straightforward job to manage a fully functional kitchen in a busy restaurant, what are the factors to be kept in mind while managing a restaurant kitchen?

Manage a restaurant kitchen: A restaurant kitchen is the powerhouse of any restaurant establishment. Kitchen management is directly linked to a **restaurant's profitability.** Let's look at some of the ways you can manage your restaurant's kitchen. And do so efficiently.

Inventory and stock management: Your restaurant kitchen inventory list gives you a brief of everything that goes into making the food. Basically, the raw materials and ingredients. A detailed inventory list helps manage food costs while making sure that only fresh products are used in the kitchen. Inventory management dictates a huge part of kitchen management solution.

- Logically **group different food ingredients** so that they're easy to spot and use. Grains, spices, fruits, and vegetables can be kept in separate shelves Even better if the **containers for dry ingredients** are marked appropriately and grouped together.

All the dairy products and frozen items go inside the refrigerators. Make sure each member of the kitchen follows the, "First in, first out" rule.

- It's a weekend. People are rushing into your restaurants. Everything is going well until you realize you've run out of tomatoes. A major ingredient that is used for preparing various kinds of sauces. Or let's say you're out of milk.

What happens to all the pies and cakes then? Nothing is more embarrassing than telling the customers that the dish they earnestly want to eat is not available that day.

- **Always keep a track of all kitchen supplies.** Make sure you buy all those food ingredients well in time for the weekends and other busy days. Conducting regular inventory stock audits will also help you **save food costs and greatly reduce kitchen waste**. Once you have your inventory sorted, you will know exactly how much of stock you require weekly or monthly.

- Prep sheets make restaurant kitchens more orderly. It's nothing but a kitchen plan that notifies the chefs and other cooks about all the food production that's going to happen in the following week. Also includes notification regarding any ingredient shortage.
- Being from the restaurant industry, you tie-up with multiple food vendors who provide you with vegetables, meat and other ingredients that you need for your kitchen according to your requirements. **Tying up with them and placing your order well in time is very important and must be done cautiously.**

Proper equipment: You must aim to make your kitchen well-equipped, less chaotic and more streamlined. Once you have everything in place, you can focus better on cooking exceptional dishes for your customers. Chefs wouldn't have to go around the kitchen looking for, say, blenders or cooking pans. Buying quality equipment that is made of non-corrosive elements like aluminum and stainless steel, prove to last longer. Apart from this, buying commercial kitchen equipment for your restaurant helps reduce labor costs and increases overall productivity. Wondering how? It's quite straight-up.

Head and Sous chefs don't have to spend time doing the initial few steps of food preparation like, chopping the veggies, grinding tomatoes or blend a garlic paste. All this is a matter of only a few minutes, thanks for the new-age commercial kitchen equipment.

Essential tips for Scheduling: Scheduling plays a key role in restaurant kitchen management. Start a few hours prior. The initial processes of cooking in a restaurant kitchen are significant and time-consuming.

- It's always better to **plan and start well before the service in your restaurant begins.** That's the time when you can brief the head chef and sous chef who can further pass on the instructions to their team members and then start cooking. Based on customer reviews and past experiences, you can spend some time with the kitchen staff and decide mutually on new ways in which you can improve employee productivity.
- **Run the prep sheet with all your employees** at the beginning of the day or towards the end of it. This is especially important for restaurant kitchens that make everything from scratch. Create elaborate prep sheets based on sales reports. This way you'll know how much time certain dishes will take to make and who to assign those to. If anyone of the kitchen staff members has a leave scheduled for the coming week, discuss who is going to fill in for them.
- You need staff in your restaurant kitchen according to the days. To put simply, **you'd clearly need more people on weekends as compared to Mondays.** And having regular updates and insights into individual employees, you'll know exactly who to keep for longer hours and otherwise. Individual employee's track sales on your POS system will also help in the same. The workflow needs to remain undisturbed.
- **Before starting the services, make sure you have all the ingredients in place for your specials and regular menu items.** Discuss the serving procedures with the wait-staff. Things they must keep in mind, about the seasonal dishes and the regular ones, while interacting with customers.
- Staff scheduling is a critical part of restaurant kitchen management. **Keeping a track of their shifts, organizing and reorganizing their schedules on certain special days and occasions, comes under this arena of schedules.**

It also includes team outings and in-house events for the kitchen staff.

- Brace yourself for multitasking in your own restaurant kitchen. **Even though your team is well capable of handling things on their own, you might have to step in and do many of the tasks yourself.** For example, you might have to plate the dishes before they're sent out to the customers.

Or make a gin and tonic, if the bartender is busy with other customers on a Saturday night. This will encourage other members to work even harder.

Plan your kitchen layout: If you're just starting out, constructing and executing a "kitchen plan" makes sense. It falls under systematic kitchen management solutions. Your kitchen plan is nothing but the blueprint of your entire restaurant kitchen. Given below are the various segments of a restaurant kitchen plan.

1. **Kitchen layout:** All back-of-house operations are executed in the restaurant kitchen so one can only imagine the high-pressure environment. Therefore, it becomes important to **equally divide different prep stations and counters so that no two operations are disturbed.**

Apart from this, the kitchen layout would also include things like the total number of wash stations, air ventilation, areas for commercial kitchen and safety equipment and more.

1. **Storage:** Next comes storage. There must be designated areas for storing kitchen equipment and stock. That not only makes the kitchen look more organized but also makes it easier for the chefs and other cooks to fetch these while cooking. Avoid crowding your kitchen. Replace those 2-3 bulky pieces of equipment with a single one that performs multiple functions. For example, a blender does the basic functions of chopping, slicing, grinding and more, making the functions of knives redundant and unnecessary. Going vertical always makes sense when it comes to storing those long handle pans, spoons, knives, etc. Fixing shelves and racks on kitchen walls help in decongesting the storerooms.

3. **Stock needs:** You need to decide on your restaurant menu and it's only then that you would know the ingredients for them. Your restaurant POS system when integrated with an inventory system will you complete visibility into your stock purchase. The inventory contains many perishable items and your inventory sheet will help prevent unnecessary purchases or over ordering. Everything can be tracked accurately.

4. **Guidelines on staff roles, food preparation, and kitchen sanitation:** You must have set guidelines for your kitchen staff regarding their respective jobs and common rules that apply to everyone working inside.

A mutually decided procedure must be followed by all chefs and cooks before they start preparing the food. Basic sanitary practices like washing/sanitizing hands before entering the kitchen and cooking food. All these sets of rules must be decided beforehand so that once the restaurant kitchen is functional, it runs well and without any errors.

5. **Number of staff for operations:** A list of all the employees you would require to run the kitchen. Right from chefs to prep cooks and servers. You must have a clear layout of their respective roles and areas inside the restaurant kitchen.

Methods of Cooking

Baking: This involves applying a dry convection heat to your food in an enclosed environment.

The dry heat involved in the baking process makes the outside of the food go brown, and keeps the moisture locked in.

Baking is regularly used for cooking pastries, bread and desserts.

Frying: This means cooking your food in fat – there are several variations of frying:

- Deep-frying, where the food is completely immersed in hot oil
- Stir-frying, where you fry the food very quickly on a high heat in a oiled pan
- Pan-frying, where food is cooked in a frying pan with oil; and Sauteing, where the food is browned on one side and then the other with a small quantity of fat or oil.

Frying is one of the quickest ways to cook food, with temperatures typically reaching between 175 – 225°C.

Roasting: Roasting is basically a high heat form of baking, where your food gets drier and browner on the outside by initial exposure to a temperature of over 500F.

This prevents most of the moisture being cooked out of the food.

The temperature is then lowered to between 425 and 450F to cook through the meat or vegetables.

Grilling: This is a fast, dry and very hot way of cooking, where the food is placed under an intense radiant heat. You can use various sources of heat for grilling: wood burning, coals, gas flame, or electric heating.

Before grilling, food can be marinaded or seasoned.

A similar method to grilling is broiling, where the heat source originates from the top instead of the bottom.

Steaming: This means cooking your food in water vapour over boiling water. For this, it's handy to have a steamer, which consists of a vessel with a perforated bottom placed on top of another containing water.

Steam rises as the water boils, cooking the food in the perforated vessel above.

Poaching: This involves a small amount of hot liquid, ideally at a temperature between 160 and 180F. The cooking liquid is normally water, but you can also use broth, stock, milk or juice. Common foods cooked by poaching include fish, eggs and fruit.

Simmering: This involves cooking liquid on top of a stove in a pot or pan. It should be carried out on a low heat, and you will see bubbles appearing on the surface of the liquid as your dish cooks.

Broiling: Similar to grilling, the heat source comes directly from the top. You should be able to adjust your oven setting to broiling, but be careful, as this cooking methods works quickly and your meal could easily become burned.

Favorite dishes for broiling include chicken, beef and fish.

Blanching: Here the food is part-cooked, and then immediately submerged in ice cold water to stop the cooking process. All sorts of vegetables can be blanched, including green beans, asparagus and potatoes.

Braising: First the food is sauted or seared, and then simmered in liquid for a long period of time until tender. Pot roasts, stews and casseroles can be cooked in this way if they contain larger food items such as poultry legs.

Stewing: Again, the food is sauted or seared first, and then cooked in liquid, but normally uses smaller ingredients such as chopped meats or vegetables.

PLATING TECHNIQUE

Conceptualize plating as an art form: you are the artist; the plate is your canvas, and the food is your medium. Master the following plating techniques to perfect your craft.

Key Considerations: When you see an experienced chef plating an exquisite artwork onto a plate, it's understandable if you feel overwhelmed at the idea of trying to do the same at your restaurant. But if you break it down, there are a few key skills, techniques, and general principles which make the whole world of food presentation and styling less daunting.

Color: Food naturally tells us when it's fresh, ripe, and ready to eat with its vibrancy. We can use this natural trait to our advantage by using vibrant colors, blocks of color, or color contrasts to make a plate more appealing and interesting.

Arrangement: Whether you opt for a precision approach or a rustic style, the arrangement of the food on the plate is all-important to how the diner perceives it. Arranging your main ingredient, accompaniments, sauces, and garnishes in an attractive way forms the foundation for a well-presented dish.

Texture: Texture is an important component in how a dish is enjoyed, but it also changes the way a plate looks. Aim for a mix of textures and layers to add accents and interest to your plates.

Balance: Balance doesn't just mean plating food symmetrically or evenly across the plate. Just as your dish should have a harmony of salty, sour, and sweet flavors, the plate should look balanced too. One color, texture, or element shouldn't take over and spoil the visual appeal of the dish as a whole.

How Easy it is to Eat: Above all, a plate of food should taste delicious and be enjoyable to eat. Never let any other factor get in the way of how easy it is for your guests to actually eat the food. For example, garnishes should be edible, and thought should be put into how the diner will pick up the food and what kind of plate is most appropriate.

Food Plating Techniques and Ideas: With the five key considerations in mind, we can move on to practical techniques and common food plating ideas to help you at the moment when the food actually meets the plate.

Plate Selection

First off, you have to choose what your food is going to sit on. More often than not, it's some kind of plate or bowl – although some chefs opt for slates, boards, or items like fryer baskets for serving fries.

Different shaped plates can be used to emphasize or complement a specific element of the dish:

- **Round plates** are the most familiar. They can look great with the star element in the center – or off-center – and garnishes and sauces swirled around the outside.
- **Square plates** are often used for more precise food presentation. The hard angles and straight lines can be used to emphasize precise lines and shapes in your plating.
- **Rectangular and oval plates** can be used to create an attractive line of ingredients along the plate. Or to highlight a certain ingredient, like a whole fish that matches an oval shaped plate.
- **Plate size** has a massive effect on presentation. You don't want the plate to be too small and overcrowded – but too big, and your food is lost. Large plates are often used to create white space around the food, which can look clean and stylish if done well.

Plate color alsoimpacts the look of the dish by providing a contrasting background:

- **White plates** are common for a blank canvas on which to paint your sauces and garnishes.
- **Black plates** can offer a striking contrast when used with white or brightly colored sauces and soups.
- **Charcoal, grey, or off-white** plates are also effective for color contrasts. It's uncommon to see many other colors as you usually want the ingredients themselves to contrast with the background and bring the vibrancy of color to the dish.

Plate Presentation Techniques: Selecting the right plate for your meal is the first step in the food presentation process. Consider the following to choose the ideal plate for your food presentation:

- **Plate Size** - Your plate should be big enough to make your food stand out and petite enough to prevent your portions from appearing small.
- **Light vs Dark Plates** - Use light and dark plates to make your meal stand out. White plates are popular because they offer a neutral background for brightly colored foods. Dark plates lend beautifully to light-colored dishes, such as a whitefish or creamy polenta.
- **Plate Color** - A plate's color can stimulate or reduce appetites. Red increases the appetite, so serving appetizers on red plates keeps customers interested in ordering large entrees and desserts. Professional platers consider blue dinnerware unappetizing because there are few naturally occurring blue foods.
- **Restaurant Style** - If you operate a fine dining establishment, classic China dinnerware pairs well with traditional plating styles. A trendy gastropub should invest in unique plates with unconventional shapes that facilitate maximum plating creativity.

Food Arrangement Techniques: How you arrange your food determines your meal's aesthetic tone, structural integrity, and flavor dispersion. Here are a few of the most important food arrangement techniques:

- **The Rule of Thirds** - When applied to cooking, the rule of thirds prescribes placing the focal point of your dish on either the left or right side of the plate, rather than the center. Use white space by thinking of the rim as your frame and highlight your plate's focal point(s).
- **View Your Plate as a Clock** - As you place your ingredients, picture the face of a clock. From the diner's point of view, your protein should be between 3 and 9, your starch/carbohydrate from 9 to 12, and your vegetable from 12 to 3.

- **Don't Overcrowd Your Plate** - Keep your design simple by focusing on one ingredient (usually the protein). Having a focal point helps you arrange your accompanying items to complement your standout item.
- **Moist Ingredients First** - Plate moist ingredients first and prevent them from running by topping them with other foods. For example, you can angle sliced meat against mashed vegetables.
- **Create Flavor Bites** - Flavor bites are forkfuls of food that combine all the ingredients in your dish into one bite. Flavor bites are essential to quality plating as they please both the eyes and the taste buds.
- **Mix Textures** - Contrasting a smooth vegetable puree with crunchy onion straws or topping a steak with crumbled blue cheese yields appealing texture combinations that are classic in high-end cuisine.

Visual Plating Techniques: Maximizing the visual elements of your meal is a key plating technique. While your arrangement develops around your protein, manipulating the colors and sizes of the other elements on your plate enhances your focal point and creates a gourmet presentation.

- **Serve Odd Quantities** - If you're serving small foods like shrimp, scallops, or bite-sized appetizers, always give guests odd quantities.

- **Color Diversity** - Colorful dishes build the expectation of a flavorfully complex meal before your patrons take their first bite. Add green vegetables or brightly colored fruits that contrast with your focal point.
- **Monochromatic Meals** - Plating color-coded items together visually builds the expectation that the dish only offers one flavor. When the palate receives multiple textures and flavors instead, it surprises the tastebuds, causing them to engage with the dish.
- **Add Height to Your Plate** - Stimulate your guests' eyes by building height. While compactly stacking ingredients isn't as popular as it was 5-10 years ago, building layers of food for guests to explore offers an exciting experience.
- **Create Visual Balance** - Balance your plate's landscape by leaning long, flat items against taller elements (ex: leaning asparagus spears at a 45-degree angle across a stack of lamb lollipops).

Sauce Plating Techniques: With your principal ingredients plated, you're ready to top your dish with delicious sauces that enhance your food presentation. Think of your squeeze bottle or spoon as a paintbrush, and your sauce as a medium. Once you're done adding your sauce, make sure you wipe down the edge of your plate with a towel, so no drippings distract from your presentation. We explain some of the simplest, most fail-proof sauce plating techniques below.

- **Smeared Sauce Plating Technique** - Fill a squeeze bottle with your sauce. Squeeze a thick layer of sauce and form a large, filled-in circle on your plate. Take a spoon or plating wedge and dip it into the middle of the sauce where it's thickest. Quickly pull the sauce across your plate.
- **Accent Dots Plating Technique** - Fill a squeeze bottle with your desired sauce. Analyze your plate from the perspective of the rule of thirds, then add accent dots. Use multiple sauces to create additional color contrast.

- **Smeared Accent Dots Plating Technique** - Alternate between two sauce accent dots in a curved line along the side of your plate. Then, take a small plating wedge and place it at the center of the first accent dot in your row. Drag the plating wedge through the accent dots, creating a multicolored, single-sided edge.
- **Swirled Sauce Plating Technique**- Fill a squeeze bottle with your desired sauce. Place your plate atop a cake turntable. Point your squeeze bottle face down at the center of the plate. Spin your stand while simultaneously squeezing your bottle. Adjust your wrist to vary your swirled design. You can use multiple sauces to create more visual contrast.

Garnishing Techniques: In the past, chefs casually threw a piece of kale and an orange slice onto every plate. However, these garnishes added nothing exciting to the dish, and few guests ate them. Modern garnishes pair thoughtfully with the meal to create flavor bites. Follow these garnishing techniques and guidelines to master the last step of food presentation.

- **Edible Garnishes** - As you finish plating, remember that garnishes should always be edible and enhance the dish. To determine whether a garnish belongs, ask yourself whether you would want to consume it in the same bite as the meal it accompanies.
- **Intentional Placement** - Never heap garnishes in one corner of the plate. Instead, disperse them thoughtfully to add color or texture. For example, place crispy carrot shoestrings atop a delicate filet of fish nested in a curry sauce and decorate the plate with pomegranate seeds.
- **Less Is More** - Never clutter your plate for the sake of a garnish. If your plate is full, opt for a drizzle of flavor-infused vinegar or oil to enhance the taste and appearance of your dish without overcrowding your plate.

- **Garnishes to Avoid** - Avoid using unappetizing garnishes like raw herbs, large chunks of citrus, and anything with a strong odor. Also, avoid garnishes that take a long time to apply.

Plating Tools: Having professional tools is essential for commercial plating. We've rounded up the foundational items you need to create restaurant-quality food presentations.

Decorating brushes aid in detailed line work and broad sauce strokes. You can also use decorating brushes to create a puree or coulis base for meats or vegetables.

Garnishing kits come with everything you need to garnish your signature dishes, including plating wedges, tongs, squeeze bottles, and brushes.

Molds keep plates clean and increase visual appeal by cutting ingredients to specific shapes and sizes. Ring molds help you develop height and structure when stacking ingredients.

Precision tongs help you place garnishes or small, delicate items. Many tongs feature micro-serrations for improved grip and stability.

Plating wedges come pre-cut with flat, round, or pointed edges and are perfect for smearing soft ingredients and creating sauce designs.

Shavers allow you to top your dishes with shaved or grated chocolate, hard cheese, or soft vegetables.

Plating Spoons in varying sizes are essential to the art of food presentation. Saucier spoons help you drag sauce across your plate and slotted spoons quickly separate solids from liquids.

Squeeze bottles help you apply sauce and aioli to your finished plate. Many come with adjustable precision control tips.

CHAPTER FOURTEEN

Briefing and De-briefing

We Hoteliers spend our lot of time on board while assisting guests, understanding operations and smoothing things! Yet we face many problems throughout the shift. So... Briefing and De-briefing are designed to solve problems, do brainstorming, do preparation and have work discussions with the help of effective communication.

In restaurant management, preparing each dinner service is like preparing a show where everyone has a role, there is a script to follow and an audience to impress. In this respect, there is a crucial step that you must take so that everything turns out great, so... The briefing or status meeting held by the manager or area manager with the entire team before each work day. The briefing's topics range from general aspects to more specific details, from the culinary selection to communication problems in the team. Let's say that it is a very crucial moment to ensure that things go well most of the time. It is usually held at the beginning of the week as well as every day before each dinner service.

These topics are crucial for ensuring that this meeting is truly effective:

Occupancy organisation. The key point in any briefing is to inform all the staff about the scheduled reservations and how they would be organised among the tables, the occupancy schedules, the number of diners, new and regular customers that will arrive, reservations with a discount or promotion, etc.

Assignment of tasks. This is where the manager, supervisor or area manager divides the tasks among the staff. Who will serve the tables, who will be in charge of welcoming the customers, etc? Although each person has their role, restaurant teams tend to have variations, such as staff that perform double shifts, back-up staff, etc. By assigning tasks in the briefing, each person knows their role during each dinner service, thereby preventing unnecessary improvisations.

VIP or special guests Briefings are also where you inform employees about which clients should receive more personalised or special treatment, such as major groups, influencers or food critics. In doing so, the team can understand the objective of welcoming these guests to the restaurant and the marketing campaigns that will be carried out.

For instance, familiarise yourself with an influencer's preferences in order to impress them, or find out who is the head or leader of the group of that important company whose regular business we wish to obtain.

Customer needs. Another essential topic in our status meetings are the special needs of customers that will arrive at each dinner service. Determine if there is a celiac customer, if anyone has any sort of allergy, if they do not eat meat, if they cannot consume a certain type of carbohydrate, if there is any couple that is celebrating their wedding anniversary or if there is a family with babies or small children and how they would be served in each case.

Details about the culinary selection. Of course, the food is one of the most important topics in any briefing. In this meeting, all staff must be up to date on the dishes and drinks that are available for each service, Today's Chef Special, non-availability, one-off changes for some dishes, etc.

It is also the perfect time to make sure that everyone is intimately familiar with the ingredients and their origins, cooking methods, pairings and, of course, the prices of each product so that you can respond to any questions that customers may have.

Marketing strategies. This is where staff acknowledge the active marketing campaigns, such as up-selling and cross-selling techniques to increase the sales of certain products as well as the average ticket. Other things that are acknowledged are the signature dishes that you wish to sell and key phrases or words that will be used to welcome or say goodbye to clients, for instance. You can also brush up on digital campaigns, such as inviting customers to post their opinion about their experience on Specialised portals like Google Review and TripAdvisor or using a hashtag to tag their posts on social media..

Praise and criticism. The briefing is also the perfect moment to share with the team both positive and negative opinions that have been received from customers, i.e. the complements and complaints. It is a measure that helps to improve staff performance when there are mistakes and to strengthen it when they are doing well. On the other hand, it serves to inspire other people on the team to imitate the good deeds and prevent possible restaurant management conflicts in the future.

Feedback from staff. Following the previous point, no status meeting should end without hearing the team's feedback. All staff have the right to express themselves and provide their opinion about both operational and personal matters.

This is the time to clear up misunderstandings, report any complaints about the performance of others and express each person's needs. It is also the perfect time to coordinate agendas among everyone, specify days off and days on which someone may need to leave early due to a personal emergency, etc. In the end, the briefing is to restaurant management like rehearsals are to operas, which is why it is very important to hold them and deal with all the relevant issues to ensure a magnificent performance in every dinner service. Let's hope that is the case as well in your restaurant and that your team can work at ease. Your customers will notice!

Now if we talk about De-briefing, then A debrief is a simple, yet powerful tool that enables a team to self-correct, bond as a team, and enhance their performance. During debriefs or de-briefing, team members reflect upon a recent experience, discuss what went well and identify opportunities for improvement. They attempt to build a common understanding – by clarifying roles, priorities and goals – remove obstacles to collaboration, and reach agreements about how to ensure future success.

CHAPTER FIFTEEN

Budgeting and forecasting

Your restaurant's budget and forecast are as close as you're going to get to see the future of your business. Your restaurant budget defines your financial limits, while your restaurant's financial forecast determines what you'll be able to do within those limits. While there will always be costs you can't control, a budget gives you framework for the financial decisions you can control. First, we will look at what the role of the budget is and what data we need to make it work. We will cast our eyes over the three main parts of the financial projections, and the tables that compose it. And last but not least, we will give you several tools that will help you create your own projections.

Importance of Financial Budgeting: The financial forecast allows you to assess whether or not your project is likely to be profitable. You will analyze every detail of the restaurant you have in mind (from costs to menu prices) to make sure that it's financially viable. You will also list the investments required for starting up your business, such as kitchen equipment and furniture, to set out how much money you need to get your business off the ground.

The financial forecast will also give you an idea of what you can expect over the next three years, allowing you to plan the development of your business with confidence. It's also important to remember that your restaurant's budget will be essential when you're looking for financing. You can be 100% sure that a banker or investor will ask you for these numbers when presenting your project, so make sure they're set out accurately and attractively.

Information is required to create a financial forecast: Your restaurant's financial forecast will be based on specific data that you will need to have collected beforehand. First of all, you will need to have already carried out market research to evaluate the commercial potential of your location.

The market research allows you to answer the following questions:

- How much will the average spend per head be?
- How many times per year will the average customer visit the restaurant?

- How many people are likely to visit your restaurant during opening hours?

When assessing this, think about the potential customers around you (e.g. office workers, students, families) and split it into lunch and dinner sittings during the week and on weekends.

- What are the nearby restaurants? Do they serve the same type of cuisine or do they have a very different menu from yours?

Your market analysis will also consider the marketing strategy you need to put in place to get your restaurant's name out there. Whether you set up your own website or pay people to hand out flyers on the street, these promotional costs will need to be included in your budget. Finally, you will also need to draw up a precise list of the resources needed to keep the restaurant running on a day-to-day basis. Between staff, insurance and purchasing a music license, it's important to ensure these are all accounted for if you want to create a budget that's as close to reality as possible

Sales forecast: When creating your restaurant financial projections, the first thing you should do is set out a sales forecast. Your level of inventory and staffing needs will depend on how busy you expect your restaurant to be, so it's easier to start here. To estimate your sales projections, you can begin by evaluating your restaurant's maximum capacity.

When putting together this data, it's important to bear in mind:

- The number of seats available and the amount of time each customer spends at the table.
- The restaurant's opening hours
- The time it takes the kitchen to prepare the dishes and the acceptable waiting time before they reach the table

Once you know your maximum capacity, you'll want to take a look at the occupancy rate. This assesses the percentage of tables occupied during peak and off-peak dining times. You will then need to determine how many customers are likely to visit your restaurant each day based on market research data. The last part you'll need to evaluate the average revenues per table. This will vary depending on your menu prices and the clientele targeted by your restaurant.

Overheads budget: Overheads are the expenses needed to run the business on a day-to-day basis. To make sure these figures are as precise as possible, it's important to quantify each expense item using estimates provided by your suppliers.

Generally speaking, a restaurant will have significant overhead costs in terms of payroll. You will need both kitchen and dining room staff, not to mention seasonal workers who will flow in and out during the summer or winter. It's therefore vital that you accurately estimate the number of employees you will need by taking your number of potential customers into account. Your overheads will also include rent for the premises as well as water, gas and electricity bills.

Typically, additional costs will include licensing costs, insurance, maintenance, cleaning products, and/or commissions if you use online delivery platforms.

Actual vs. Budget P & L: A P&L is usually filled up when your restaurant is already operating. What if your restaurant is still in the feasibility study phase? This is where the budget or pro forma P & L comes in. The numbers of your pro forma P & L will come from research and forecasts. Important line items such as sales, cost of goods sold, and labor cost should be forecasted in three different ways. First, a conservative forecast wherein you assume that your restaurant did not attract enough customers. Second, your expected forecast that entails your expected orders per day. Lastly, an aggressive forecast that surpasses your expectations and gives you the fastest return on investment.

Step-by-Step Guide on Restaurant Budgeting: After sharing some basics on restaurant budgeting above, it is time to show you how to do restaurant budgeting that really works.

Record and Categorize Everything: The first step in creating your restaurant budget is to get all the necessary data. You need to implement ways to organize all types of revenue and expenses the restaurant makes. The most commonly used methods are a spreadsheet in Microsoft Excel or advanced accounting software. The next step is to do category management on all your entries. We've broken down the most common entries into subcategories. See which lines fit your restaurant and add them to your tracking system.

Sales

- **Food sales**
- **Beverage sales**
  - **Liquor sales**
  - **Beer sales**
  - **Soft Beverage sales**
- **Delivery sales**
- **Event sales**

Cost of Goods Sold

- Food cost
- Beverage cost
    - Liquor cost
    - Bottled beer cost
    - Soft Beverage cost
- Delivery Sales cost
- Event cost

Cost of Labor

- Management team
- Entry level employees
- Labor benefits

Expenses

- Rental expense
- Security expense
- Utilities expense
- Royalties expense
- Marketing expense

- Insurance expense
- Permits and licenses expense
- Depreciation expense

Keep Track of your Sales Numbers: As mentioned above, we have two ways of tracking the sales number of a restaurant. First, via restaurant budgeting and forecasting when the restaurant is still non-operational. Second, via tracking the history of your sales number from previous years to make an accurate projection. In order to make an accurate projection, try to use this calculator as a guide

		Average Check	Avg. # of customers per hr	Total sales
Monday	Lunch			0
	Dinner			0
Tuesday	Lunch			0
	Dinner			0
Wednesday	Lunch			0
	Dinner			0
Thursday	Lunch			0
	Dinner			0
Friday	Lunch			0
	Dinner			0
Saturday	Lunch			0
	Dinner			0
Sunday	Lunch			0
	Dinner			0

Enter Caption

How to Use this Calculator: In this calculator, here are some of the assumptions made to get a forecasted weekly sales of a restaurant. First, you'll need to get the total front of house space so you can calculate the maximum number of customers per hour.

A safe assumption is one customer can occupy 2 sqm of space. So in this example, a 48 square meter front of house can seat around 24 people.

Next, you'll need to determine your operating hours and separate them into lunch and dinner. This will depend on the type of restaurant you own but for the sake of an example, let us assume that it's a full service restaurant that offers different menus for lunch and dinner. If your restaurant serves breakfast, make sure to add a row per day named "Breakfast". Count the number of hours you'll serve breakfast, lunch, and dinner as you'll be using this to forecast your weekly sales.

The next step is to calculate your average check amount. Separate these into three categories: mains, sides, and drinks. In the example above, let's break down the 150 rupees average check for lunch. You can get this by averaging the prices of your mains and sides: 110 rupees for main and 40 rupees for sides. Lastly, you will need to assume the number of customers per hour that you'll be serving.

Use the maximum of 24 people as a baseline to calculate this. You can do the same thing we did the P & L above – create a column for conservative, expected, and aggressive.

For a conservative projection, use 50% of total seating capacity, 65% and 80% for expected and aggressive, respectively. Get your average customer per hour and multiply by the total number of hours you operate lunch or dinner. Afterwards, multiply the total you get to the average check and you'll get your total sales for the day. Do this until Sunday and multiply by 4.33 to get a monthly forecast. Note that we use 4.33 to get a more accurate monthly total because there's 30-31 days to a month, multiplying by 4 will only yield in 28 days.

What If you have an Existing Restaurant: If you've been operating for a certain period of time, it is most likely that you have data of your sales from the previous years. This is a good basis in projecting sales for the next year. Start off by listing down on a spreadsheet your total sales broken down into months. Then, depending on the number of years you're operating, separate them into columns

	2018	2019	2020	2021	2022
January					
February					
March					
April					
May					
June					
July					
August					
September					
October					
November					
December					
Total					

Enter Caption

In the restaurant business, not all months will have the same revenue. There are months in the year where it's peaking while there's also months where it's very lean. Use these historical data to your advantage and provide a good projection for the next year. For example, your restaurant usually does well during the weekends and festival time. Make sure to take this into account when putting up a projected sales number.

List Down All Expenses: As we've mentioned in step 1, listing down all your expenses and categorizing them can help you prepare in restaurant budgeting. Fixed expenses, like rent, are costs that you cannot change. On the other hand, variable expenses are costs that you can set a budget on. Electricity and water are two expenses that a restaurant can save expenses on. Try to set a budget that's reasonable to achieve for the team. In addition, maintenance and repairs are sort of an added cost for the restaurant.

Try to set strict rules in taking care of equipment, accessories and other small wares to limit this type of expense. The expenses file should always be updated every end of day.

This is to ensure that you don't miss anything. In addition, this file also serves as the file that you can send to accountants for filing tax returns.

Conduct a Sales vs. Cost Analysis: It is now time to put it all together. Conducting an analysis on both your sales and costs will give you an idea on how your restaurant is faring. For example, if you see your sales at 200,000 and your total expenses at 150,000. What do you think this means? It means your restaurant is healthy enough that it's earning 50,000. On the other hand, if your sales are at 200,000 and your total expenses are at 250,000, changes might have to be made with your restaurant. Because if this keeps up, the days of the restaurant might be numbered.

Don't Be Afraid to Make Drastic Changes: Once the restaurant's expenses have surpassed its sales, it might be time to revisit some things in the restaurant. The most common culprit is the high cost of goods sold. Study and research all possible ingredients that you can use for your menu with the goal of minimizing food costs. Aside from a high COGS, a high number of employees can also be a problem. A bigger problem is if these employees are unproductive and offer poor customer service. These will turn your customers off and might not give an opportunity for them to come back. In short, make sure you hire the right staff so avoid having the poor customer service label.

Define Your Costs: The nice thing about restaurant costs is that many of them are fixed. Fixed costs don't change, making them easier to anticipate and include in your budget. But you'll also have to account for semi-variable costs, which will change slightly from month to month. Then there's non-fixed costs, which are guaranteed to change every month. You'll need to include some padding in your budget based on your previous year's restaurant expenses, so that you can project these to a degree of accuracy.

Here's the breakdown of the kinds of costs you'll need to define for your budget.

Fixed costs: Costs that won't change.

Examples: insurance, rent, loan payments

Semi-fixed/semi-variable cost: Costs that are guaranteed but can vary every month.

Examples: salaries, hourly pay, utility bills, food costs, small wares replacements, take out supplies

Non-fixed/variable costs: Costs that respond directly to changes in the restaurant and sales volume.

Example: Repairs, marketing, advertising, taxes, delivery charges

When you're budgeting, it also helps to know costs you can control versus what you can't. By defining these costs, you can determine your must-haves against your nice-to-haves.

Controllable costs: Costs you can control.

Examples: labor, marketing, food cost

Uncontrollable costs: Costs you can't control.

Example: rent, property taxes, other occupancy costs

Calculate Your Breakeven Point: Now that you've projected your total costs and expected sales for the year, it's wise to calculate your breakeven point – which will ultimately tell you if you're set to make a profit. Restaurant profit can only occur when sales exceed the breakeven point.

The formula for calculating profit is: Sales – (Labour + Food costs + Overhead)

Budgeting and Forecasting Mistakes

Failing to budget for marketing: Marketing is responsible for generating buzz, your brand identity, and filling seats. Your marketing budget is an investment in the growth of your business – so don't skip out on this line item just because it's not directly related to your operations. Marketing is considered a controllable cost, so if sales are slim one month, you can react by cutting your marketing budget. But don't be cheap over the long haul: it's recommended that 3%–6% of your monthly revenue should go towards marketing.

Over-forecasting sales: We know: you want to see huge sales growth. We want that for you, too. But over-forecasting sales only leads to disappointment and disaster. When you overestimate your revenue, your cost percentages won't be realistic – which may result in overspending. And when you fall short on your sales goals, you risk causing panic in the workplace and disappointing investors.

To avoid this, base your forecasts and projections on conservative trends.

Failing to engage management: If your management staff are unaware of your financial status and processes, they won't know how to effectively order inventory or schedule staff. Communicate your budget to your management staff so that they're aware of your restaurant's cost limitations. Also, if you've hired the right people, they'll be able to take a proactive approach in making decisions that are right for your business. So trust your people!

Ignoring external factors: Street closures, neighborhood block parties, festivals, bad weather, minimum wage increases (including tipped minimum wage), food cost increases: each affects your sales and costs.

Always account for variable change. It's good practice to keep up with your local chamber of commerce, labor laws, and community newspaper so that you can anticipate external factors that impact sales and costs.

Not using software: Manual, spreadsheet-based tactics are about as useful today as a columnar pad. Use POS software that seamlessly integrates with your accounting software, so that you're not vulnerable to errors. Make sure you have the ability to pull reports in real time so you can make quick decisions about your business.

CHAPTER SIXTEEN

Restaurant Reports

It takes a lot to run a successful restaurant. While offering good food and great customer experience is essential, you also need to constantly analyze and work upon the strengths and weaknesses to stay ahead of the competition. This is where the role of data and reporting and analytics come into the picture. While most restaurant POS software provides multiple restaurant reports, it is important to know the most crucial reports that you need to monitor on day to day basis. Restaurant reports will enable you to keep a very keen eye on all your restaurant operations and make the necessary changes in the fields which are not performing that well, which will further boost your business.

Restaurant Sales Report: Sales report should consist of the comprehensive data of the total sales that happened at your restaurant on a particular day. It should tell you the total number of bills generated and the discounts conferred. If you are running multiple outlets, then the report should give you the data of all the outlets in one central place. This will help you compare the sales happening across all the outlets. Such comprehensive data will help you to understand what works the best for different outlets and take steps accordingly to bolster your total sales across all the outlets.

Inventory Report: Since it is the raw materials that help you run your restaurant and since it is the inventory where internal thefts are rampant, it becomes necessary for you to keep a check on your inventory rather closely. An inventory report should tell you in details the beginning and the closing inventory of each item, the amount of each item used on a particular day across all the outlets. Inventory report also includes the Variance Report that tells you the difference between the actual stock consumption and Ideal stock consumption. A Variance of 3-5% is acceptable, however, anything over this implies that wastage or even internal pilferage may be happening at your restaurant.

Menu Performance Reports: Analyzing menu performance reports would not just give you deep insights about your business, but also help you understand what your customers are liking about your restaurant. You can identify the items that are contributing the most to the sales, and the items that are not popular with the customers.

Based on these reports, you can eliminate and add new items on the menu to boost sales. By removing the items that are not generating sales, you will be able to reduce your Food Costs, and the operating costs involved in preparing those items and maintaining inventory.

Expense Reports: Unexpended expenses crop up, every day, and this makes it all the more important to keep track of all the expenses keeping in mind the fixed cost, that will help you maintain some budget at the standby.

Hence, an expense report must include, the rents, the electricity, phone, wifi, water bills, the salaries of your staff, costs of the inventory, the maintenance of the equipment, the budget required for hosting different events, and the miscellaneous expenses include the replacement for the broken crockery, the spoilt tablecloth and the like. An expense report should give you a comprehensive understanding of all the expenses that your restaurant incurs on a daily basis and over a period of time.

The importance of having this report is, you can allocate your budget well, and know where exactly you need to cut down. This will help you reduce unnecessary expenses, which will bolster your overall profit.

CRM Reports: Keeping a comprehensive CRM database will help you have all your customer reports at one central place. Since the retention of customers is more important than increasing the customer trial base, CRM reports will come in handy. The CRM reports will tell you about the customer orders, the date and time of visits, and the bill generated at the table. This will help you understand the best and the least selling items, and accordingly, you can sit with your chef and do your menu engineering. It will also help you to tap the customers who you think has the potential of becoming your loyal customers. Harping on the customer data you can run loyalty programs, or you can run robust marketing campaigns; that will help you in customer retention.

Performance Reports: If you are running multiple restaurant brands and outlets, monitoring operations and keeping track of the sales can be very difficult. Consolidating reports from different sources, and relying on the restaurant manager for updates hampers decision-making.

Staff Performance Reports: Analyzing the performance of your staff is also critical if you want to run a successful restaurant business. You can set individual goals and Key Performance Indicators (KPI) for each staff member and measure their productivity on a weekly and monthly basis.

You can create these KPIs basis the restaurant reports generated from the POS software. For instance, you can set a goal for the kitchen staff to keep the Food Cost under a certain percentage. Similarly, you can measure the productivity of your wait staff by analyzing the number of tables served, total sales in a week, etc.

Restaurant reports give you a detailed understanding of your restaurant business and enable you to make data-driven decisions. All these reports must be able to give you real-time data. And you will be able to fetch these data from any part of the world, using any device. Such technology will help you to control the complete restaurant operations remotely as well.

Inventory Report: Keeping up with your restaurant's inventory means that you track, update, and monitor your stock regularly. It's an essential part of running a restaurant.

From knowing what's in your pantry to how many bottles you have in the bar, inventory reports let you know how well your restaurant's performing, and what you need to do to fine tune your business success. Inventory management lets you know about your stock, how your staff is performing, how well your dishes are selling, and which are the most profitable. These inventory reports can also prevent waste and focus your attention to improvements that grow your business. They will help you keep an organized business, and let you oversee a busy and hectic environment with reliable numbers.

Restaurant inventory composes your "cost of goods sold" (COGS), which is the cost of creating all of the items on your menu. Here is the equation to find your COGS:

COGS = Beginning Inventory + Purchased Inventory - Ending Inventory

COGS is also part of the equation to determine your net profit. Here is the equation to determine your profit and loss statement:

Net Profit = Gross Profit (Total Sales-COGS) - Labor Cost + Total Operating Cost

By analyzing the net profit equation above, we can see that a lower overall COGS means that less will be subtracted from your total sales. This in turns means that there will be more to multiply your gross profit by, ultimately leading to a higher net profit.

Type of inventories

1. Restaurant Crockery and Cutlery inventory "Monthly"
2. Kitchen Fresh, Meat and Poultry , Frozen , Dry store inventory :" Daily"

Glossary

- **Back of House:** Refers to the area of a restaurant where guests are not allowed. The kitchen, dishwashing area, and wait station are the back of the house.
- **Bar-back:** An assistant to the bartender. A bar-back usually runs glasses through the dishwasher, stocks the coolers and liquor bottles, and pours beer, wine, and non-alcoholic drinks for the waitstaff. A bar-back can also double as a busser (below).
- **Bussing:** Term used for clearing off and resetting tables after guests have left. In busier restaurants, this is done by the busboy, also called a busser.
- **Chaffing Dish:** Typically used on buffets, they are a metal dish filled with water and kept warm with a candle or fuel cell underneath.

- **Eight-Six:** If the kitchen runs out of a particular dish, the dish is "86."
- **Expediter:** The kitchen staff who group plated food together by table number for the servers to deliver.
- **Front of House:** Refers to the area of a restaurant where guests are allowed. The dining room and bar are the front of the house.
- **Host/Hostess:** The person who meets the guests and shows them to their tables. The host is also responsible for keeping track of reservations and waiting lines.
- **In the Weeds:** A term that means it is extremely busy. For example, if the kitchen has several orders across the board and are having a hard time keeping up, they are "in the weeds."

- **Line:** The line is the area that divides the cooks from the waitstaff. It is where the food is placed to await pickup.
- **Mise en Place:** Refers to the set up of the sauté station. Essentially, it means everything in its place. Most cooks put certain ingredients in a certain spot each shift, like salt and pepper to the right, olive oil to the left.
- **Plating:** Arranging the food on the plate. This includes adding any sauce or garnish before handing over to the expeditor or the server.
- **Point of Sale (POS):** A point of sale system is a computer system that helps businesses track sales. It also tracks employee sales and which dishes are sold most often.
- **On the Fly:** When something unexpected has to be cooked urgently, like when a mistake is made in an order or additional items are needed.
- **Sections:** Most restaurant dining rooms are divided into sections, and each section goes to particular waitstaff each shift.
- **Sharking:** Luring an employee from one restaurant to another.
- **Turnover Rate:** How fast tables empty and fill during a shift. A high turnover rate means more people have eaten and gone, while a slow turnover rate means the same people have been at the tables for a long time, or the table is sitting empty.

Printed by Libri Plureos GmbH in Hamburg,
Germany